Labor Relations for the Practitioner

To my wife Janet
without whose inspiration this volume
would not have come to print

Labor Relations
for the Practitioner

by
Walter E. Baer

McFarland & Company, Inc., Publishers
Jefferson, North Carolina, and London

Also by Walter E. Baer

Arbitration for the Practitioner (McFarland, 1988)
Collective Bargaining: Custom and Practice (McFarland, 1989)

British Library Cataloguing-in-Publication data available.

Library of Congress Cataloguing-in-Publication Data

Baer, Walter E.
   Labor relations for the practitioner / by Walter E. Baer.
     p. cm.
   Bibliography: p. 177.
   Includes index.
   ISBN 0-89950-401-9 (lib. bdg. : 50# alk. paper) ∞
   1. Collective labor agreements—United States. 2. Labor laws and
legislation—United States. I. Title.
KF3408.B33 1989
344.73'01—dc19
[347.3041]
                                 88-34179
                                    CIP

McFarland & Company, Inc., Publishers
  Box 611, Jefferson, North Carolina 28640

Table of Contents

Preface

The job of administering the labor agreement falls on the shoulders of practitioners on both sides of the labor-management table. Line foremen, supervisors, superintendents, personnel and industrial relations people, even lawyers from the management side become involved in the contract's interpretation and administration. On the union side there are stewards and grievance committeemen, local and international officials, and labor lawyers and other attorneys. To accomplish this task of interpretation and administration and more effectively equip these practitioners to competently represent their parties' respective interests, each side must meet a responsibility to provide its agents with the proper knowledge, concepts and attitudes to meet this objective. Usually most of these practitioners would not personally participate in the negotiation of the contract, nor would they share in the drafting of any of its many provisions.

One of the primary obligations of each respective party is to provide its practitioners with a working knowledge of the labor agreement, its interpretation, administration and implementation.

But in today's industrial situations, it is no longer sufficient for a practitioner to merely have an acquaintanceship with the labor agreement. Before this is even possible, the practitioner must also have been introduced to a variety of valid, relevant and insightful labor relations concepts and principles in order to adequately and correctly achieve labor agreement comprehension. He must be acquainted with the contractual grievance procedure, its purpose and function, and with the role his constituency expects him to play in its administration. He must be familiar with the several components which comprise the labor contract, their intent, purpose and how they may interact, and the fundamental way in which sophisticated labor relations professionals and labor arbitrators view the interpretation of the agreement. He must be aware of the weight and effect of past practice and precedent in giving meaning to, or even altering the terms and meaning of that labor contract. He must understand the importance of, and definition of, "just cause" and its specific and compelling relevance to discipline and discharge transactions. And certainly, he must be familiar with the duties and responsibilities, the latitude and freedom accorded, and the rights and obligations of the union representatives who function under the labor agreement. To many practitioners, the labor agreement is like any other legal document. To the non-lawyer layman, it is a confusing, tangled aggragation of words and phrases which can only be understood by its professional draftsmen, and sometimes, not even by them. The purpose of this work is to put into understandable terms and depictions those contractual factors which make the agreement work and hang together, and which are most often not comprehended by the practitioners.

In this connection, this volume is intended to serve a dual purpose. In addition to the enlightenment it hopefully brings, it can also serve as a document used in the training of all those practitioners, on both sides of the labor-management table, who have some labor relations responsibility and function.

1. Management Rights

Presumably the labor contract contains what represents the sole and complete embodiment of the commitments each party, the company and the union, has made to the other for the duration of its term. But no contract, no matter how comprehensive, can explicitly and fully cover all situations.

Of course, managements commonly adopt and practice a "residual rights theory" of managing. In principle, what this concept consists of, as far as a management is concerned, is that the employer has all rights it possessed prior to the coming of the union and prior to the existence of any labor agreement. In other words, *only to the extent* that the labor agreement limits, restricts or prohibits by some expressed provision management's prerogatives, is it so restricted. Therefore, it continues to possess all of the powers and functions that management would otherwise be free to exercise if no union was on the premises. Generally speaking, the ritual of collective bargaining gives the union an opportunity, legally and statutorily provided, to convince the company to accept limitations upon the exercise of certain of its previously unrestricted managerial freedoms and authorities. Where the union fails to attempt or fails to obtain such limitations on management's rights, the employer continues to possess all such remaining rights undiminished. The residual rights theory holds that the employer retains the residue of all rights it has not bargained away—those continue to reside in management.

This concept is often argued by managements, before arbitrators, particularly on issues where the union claims support for its position based on some alleged past practice. Where the union is seeking to obtain a benefit and it cannot discover supporting language to its case from the agreement, it typically resorts to a claim of past practice. Often such a claim is soundly based. Where the contract is entirely silent on the matter in dispute, it often brings to the forefront managements' argument on residual rights. The company will often assume the position that it is incumbent upon the union to establish that a contract violation has occurred by insisting it point to specific contract phrasing on the subject. Such contention by the employer is based on the premise that absent contractual provision which prohibits, restricts, limits, or somehow regulates management has preserved such freedom and right ungoverned.

Also, it is true that the preponderance of arbitral opinion holds to the following view on an employer's residual rights: "It is now a well-established generalization that every employer continues to have all powers, previously had or exercised by employers unless such powers have been curtailed or eliminated by statute or by contract with a union...."[1]

While this is generally true and fairly typical of the concept endorsed by a majority of arbitrators, it is nonetheless a generalization and there are exceptions.

A silent contract, that is, one which does not provide coverage to a given subject, *does not necessarily dictate* that any or all uncovered subjects are automatically left to management's sole discretion. Therefore it does not mean that any disputes which arise over matters not covered by pertinent contract language will always be resolved in the company's favor. Where this occurs, the customs and practices of the parties during the term of that agreement, and perhaps prevailing under prior agreements as well, may constitute a significant or *even controlling* factor in an arbitrator's final decision over the dispute.

There is no question that the presence of a written agreement imposes certain limitations on an employer's previously unfettered prerogatives. It should be recognized equally as readily that the existence of certain practices and customs under the written instrument may also provide additional limitations on management's rights not expressly indicated by the contract's wording.

A concept which is difficult for supervisors to comprehend involves the question of what the company gets from its labor agreement.

It gets but one thing. And, it gets that one thing only if it is successful in obtaining it during collective bargaining. Unfortunately, there are some employers who fail to obtain even this one thing—the no-strike clause; for them, they get nothing out of their contract with the union.

Prior to the negotiation of the labor agreement, meaning, prior to the advent of the union into the employer-employee relationship, management possessed all rights unabridged, and could establish, change and/or re-establish any wages, hours or working conditions it desired—so long as they conformed with any applicable state or federal laws or statutes. As long as they operated within the law, the employer could move wages upward, or downward, unilaterally, without conferring with employees or their representatives; they could change the number of holidays—if any—adding to or taking away as they saw fit in their sole judgment. They could provide vacations, paid sick leave, insurance, funeral leave, cost-of-living improvements, rest periods, wash-up time, and a host of others — or they could discontinue any or all of these — or add to or subtract from any at their sole discretion. Hours of work could be changed, benefits suspended or withdrawn, disciplinary suspensions or even discharges issued without a requirement of meeting a standard of just cause. Employees might be laid off or recalled, transferred, promoted or demoted, without regard for length of service or other seniority consideration. All of these and more could be done, unilaterally and freely, for no regulatory constraints impinged upon the employers' unfettered authority. Now, this is not to say that, therefore, all employers consequently decided and acted capriciously and without regard for employees' needs and desires. It is to say, they could. Management, therefore, gets nothing out of a labor agreement, since it possessed it all prior to the existence of the agreement — with but one exception: the no-strike clause of the contract, if it is obtained by the company in the give-and-take of collective bargaining.

Prior to the existence of the union contract, the employer's unorganized workers could, under law, engage in lawful work stoppages and other concerted action taking the form of economic force, in labor disputes with the employers. Therefore, prior to the coming of the union contract containing a no-strike article, the employer had no pledge or assurance from his workers of continuity of operations being maintained. The no-strike clause gives him that one thing he formerly did not have.

All other provisions of the contract operate as a prohibition, a restriction, a limitation or a regulation on those rights the subjects cover, which were previously the employer's without prohibition, restriction, limitation or regulation. In many cases, they solidify or give rigidity to the wages, benefits and working conditions which will be enjoyed by the workers during the terms of the contract.

No longer can the employer add to or subtract from, unilaterally, the number of holidays to be granted, nor the many other benefits, such as vacations, insurance, funeral pay, rest periods, paid sick leave, and the like. It probably now must (post-contract) follow some detailed procedure when it lays off, recalls, transfers, promotes or demotes — and more than likely, must consider employees' length of service in its treatment of employees in these connections.

And, most consequentially, it can no longer decide and act unilaterally, except in those few areas it has managed to preserve to itself the authority to do so — but even then, management's decisions and actions are subject to the challenge or the question of a work force now organized to speak concertedly. And, even there, where management can still function without prior bilateral intercourse, it is obliged to answer and justify its unilateral decision.

Nevertheless, it must be realized that it is a substantial compromise for the union to agree to give management its desired no-strike article.

The unions' most effective weapon is the use of, or the threat to use, economic force. They realize that without it their ability to persuade the employer on any given issue that may arise during the contract's term may be markedly impaired. The industrial plant is a dynamic community in which changes frequently occur. Job and work situations may be altered from time to time, decisions made, and actions taken which do not have the unanimous accord of all employees. When differences of opinion occur between management representatives, employees, and union officials, there must be some means by which those employees and union representatives can protest the company's decisions and actions. Without a prohibition on employees' right to strike, their protests against management's decisions can manifest themselves in various forms. Production output may be controlled and reduced; quality standards may be lowered or disregarded; or employees may totally withhold their productive labor and effort by walking out, sitting down, and so on. Needless to say, these are effective means by which the union and the employees can capture and hold management's attention to the subject of their distress. They fully realize this. To give it up is a significant compromise from their point of view.

Nevertheless, the basic promise a union can give to an employer in return for the many promises it receives in a labor agreement, is that there will be no strikes. The right to strike is what the union has as a bargaining tool and is the only thing it has to give up as consideration for the agreement. Unless this single promise flows from the bargaining agent to the employer, the labor contract cannot be considered a true bilateral exchange of promises.

The no-strike pledge enables the employer to make plans. Commitments can be made and deliveries scheduled on the assumption of uninterrupted production for the period of the contract. A strike in breach of this basic commitment denies to the employer the sole consideration bargained for and frustrates the economic purpose of the agreement from the employer's point of view.[2]

To summarize: the basic principle of the residual rights concept is to the effect that except as management has agreed to restrict the exercise of its usual functions, it retains the same rights which it possessed before engaging in collective bargaining.

The basic philosophy which the company should hold to is that the job of management is to manage. The operation of the enterprise at its maximum efficiency is management's responsibility and obligation. If a management believes in discharging these obligations, it must retain in full measure the so-called prerogative of management. It has the right to refuse to agree in collective bargaining to restrict these rights. If management agrees to limit or restrict certain of its rights through collective bargaining, the agreement should clearly define how far it has agreed to go in this direction.

The question might well be asked as to why it is necessary to have any management's rights clause in the labor agreement if the principle of residual rights is established. If there were no other reason, the fact that unions have either directly opposed, or sought to evade this concept, would alone provide sufficient justification for inclusion of a statement of management rights in the contract. The reason for the inclusion of a management's rights clause falls into three general categories:

1. Recent decisions of the courts particularly the Warrior Gulf Navigation Company case decided by the U.S. Supreme Court was to the effect that unless an item or subject is specifically excluded from the area of arbitration in a labor agreement, it is arbitrable per se. Whether the company agrees or not with this decision, it must constantly re-examine its labor agreements in the light of this Supreme Court doctrine. Assuming that in the future under this doctrine, it may be required to arbitrate matters which have either never been discussed in negotiations and subsequently dropped, its case will be materially strengthened if there is a sound management's rights clause in the agreement.

2. The principle that management retains all rights except those specifically covered by other provisions of the agreement needs expression to assist both union as well as management representatives in training subordinate stewards or supervisors in the nature of the collective bargaining agreement and in the proper performance of their duties.

3. As a practical matter, it is a significant advantage to an arbitrator to be able to cite or quote explicit language in a labor agreement in making an award, rather than to rely on an unexpressed principle.

The underlying approach of organized labor has probably best been expressed by Arthur Goldberg, then Chief Counsel for the United Steel Workers, who made the following statement when speaking to the National Academy of Arbitrators on this subject on January 27, 1956. Mr. Goldberg said:

> To the extent that present conditions and methods for change are not revised, they are accepted. Therefore, each party has a right to assume that changes in wages, hours, or working conditions, not provided for by the contract can be made only by mutual agreement or by following practices for making changes which have existed during the collective bargaining relationship, or by virtue of management's exercise of an exclusive right (such as introduction of a new product, new machine, new material, new method of manufacture, etc.).

In further support of this thesis, Goldberg, who later became a Supreme Court justice and United States Ambassador to the United Nations, commented on the nature of labor-management relationship as follows:

> The real question that arises is, What is the Deal? Is it the contract or something more? I cannot agree that the deal includes the acceptance of the pre-union past as a guide for the future. But the practices which grow up during decades of collective bargaining relationships cannot be swept aside. They have weight which must be measured in a specific case in the light of many factors. These practices, grievance settlements, understandings, etc., inevitably represent the set of circumstances which form the backdrop of the negotiation of the current agreement.

It is for the precise reason of the prevalence of this viewpoint among representatives of organized labor, that it is important that management negotiate not only the inclusion of a sound management's rights clause, but a security clause with respect to past practice. It is imperative that supervisors clearly understand that it is the implicit right of management to take action as it deems necessary and desirable, and that the only proper action of the union is to protest the action through the grievance procedure rather than to raise the question as to whether or not management has the right to act at all. As Goldberg himself said in the same address to the National Academy of Arbitrators,

> The union has a duty, and as a union man the employee has the duty as well as the right, to challenge the company's acts when they violate the workers' rights. That challenge is made through the grievance procedure, not through rebellion.[3]

Fortunately, arbitrators have tended to lean more toward the management viewpoint of management rights (the residual or reserved rights concept) as expressed earlier, rather than toward the union viewpoint as enunciated by Goldberg. However, it must be recognized that they have not embraced this position as being binding in all respects and under all circumstances.

Almost universally, arbitrators will scrutinize with care and will frequently set aside an action by management, if they are convinced that management's action is either (1) not made in good faith and with sound purpose and/or (2) served by intent or effect to nullify other provisions of the agreement.

To most employers, "the right to manage" has a basic and concrete significance. It means the right and the ability of management to take such action as the needs of the business demand without extensive and time-consuming haggling with the union over the managerial decision itself, and without having an arbiter decide after the fact (and without regard to what is or what isn't in the contract) that management had no right to make that business decision and to take that essential action.

If it could be summed up in a single word what management is concerned about — what it must have if it's to run the business at a profit, which, like it or not, is the name of the game in our society — it is flexibility to meet the competitive needs of the enterprise. For without that there would soon be no enterprise, no jobs, and, for that matter, no management, no employees, no unions — no arbitrators even.

If it could be summed up in a single word, or perhaps two words, what the union's concern is, it would be "job security." Unions are concerned, and it is their business and their right to be concerned, over the job security of their members. When all is said and done, fringe benefits are meaningless and it's up to management to recognize that concern, just as it's up to unions to recognize management's concern over flexibility. So, we're not talking here about some sterile, abstract principle, but a fundamental need of those charged with doing the management job. It is also merely realistic to state that it is incumbent on both sides to recognize that these two concerns are in fundamental conflict. To whatever extent one prevails in a given situation the other must yield. This is a fact of our industrial way of life, a necessary friction in the marriage between free enterprise and collective bargaining, and it should be recognized for what it is: a legitimate conflict of interest built into our system.

It isn't the result of the union's deliberately setting out to oust management from its job or to run the business. Unions aren't out — consciously at least — to take over the business or grab a partnership in the running of it — at least most of them are not; management should recognize this. Unions, for their part, should recognize that every management effort to obtain more flexibility, or to retain what flexibility it has, isn't an attempt to undermine or destroy the union. It isn't, and it only clouds the issue and makes a sound working relationship impossible when each side misunderstands the reason for the conflict, and attributes only the basest of motives to its opposite number.

While the differences between the viewpoints of management and labor as expressed above are obviously widely divergent, there are at least on the margins, certain areas in which it may be possible for some agreement. From purely practical considerations, there are many occasions when it is to the advantage of management to give union officers advance notice of certain management actions (while still preserving management's right to take actions) which are going to significantly affect a number of employees. The line between timely information and discussion on the one hand, and the area of negotiation on the other, is oftentimes a fine one, and it requires a rather sophisticated viewpoint on the part of management and union representatives to clearly understand, under all circumstances, the distinction between the two. In fact, there are some areas, such as in the matter of plant removal, where the National Labor Relations Board requires, as a point of doctrine, that management give advance information to a union.

With respect to those matters where the viewpoint of organized labor approaches, at least in part, that of management, in the same paper where he made the above quoted statement, Goldberg has this to say:

> When a contract says that management has the exclusive right to manage the business, it obviously refers to the countless questions which arise and are not covered by wages, hours, and working conditions, such as determination of products, equipments, materials prices, etc. Not only does management have the general right to manage a business, but many agreements provide that management has the exclusive right to direct working forces, and usually to lay off, recall, discharge, hire, etc.
>
> The right to direct where it involves wages, hours, or working conditions is a procedural right ... it is a recognition of the fact that somebody must be boss; somebody has to run the plant. People can't be wandering around at loose ends each deciding what to do next ... to assure order, there is a clear procedural line drawn: the company directs and the union grieves when it objects.

Here at least we see by implication a recognition of the fact that it is management who must always act, or take the initiative, and that it is the right of the union to grieve or protest the act, not to prevent the act from taking place. This would appear to be obvious to all; but we all too frequently see situations where a foreman's decision to take a certain course of action is challenged by a union steward as to where in the contract does management obtain the right to take such action. All too often at this point, supervisors are prone to engage in a discussion, which is in effect a negotiation, and then to come to their superiors or to the personnel department and complain that they cannot get union agreement to carry out the act. An illustration may be the best method to make the point attempted here. Typically, when a union representative believes that management has violated the labor agreement, he approaches the supervisor and asks him to point out where in the labor agreement there is a provision or a clause which gives the company the right to take the action it took. Also typically, unfortunately, in many situations, the supervisor attempts to do just that, leafing through the agreement in search of his rights to support the action taken. What each party to this conversation may not understand, and probably does not, is that the company retains and reserves to itself all rights and powers and authorities it possessed prior to the negotiation of the labor agreement except to the extent that it has restricted, limited or prohibited such rights by a provision of the contract.

The above ritual puts the shoe on the wrong foot. The fact of the matter is, it is incumbent upon the union to identify some contractual provision that prohibits, restricts, or limits management's right to take the action in the fashion in which it intends. Regarding this approach, it is desirable to distinguish the substantive burden of proof from the procedural burden of going forth with evidence. The substantive burden of proof—whether in a court of law, or an arbitration hearing, or a grievance proceeding—rests with the complaining party. It never shifts from one party to the other, and may be defined as the burden on the complaining party to prove by a preponderance of the evidence, the proof of his contentions. When the supervisor's defense is to admit all of the essential allegations of the union and to assert affirmatively that his action is justified for some other reason, then the supervisor has used an affirmative defense, and must therefore assume the substantive burden of proving the facts to sustain the defense. The word "right" means any power, privilege, or immunity, vested in one by authority, social custom or by law. "Prerogative" means the right to exercise a power or privilege in priority to, or to the exclusion of others for the exercise of which in theory there is no responsibility or accountability as to the fact and the manner of its exercise.

In recent decades there has been progressive invasion of once unchallenged areas of exclusive managerial decision. Many things which once were regarded as the right or prerogatives of management have ceased to be so characterized. Inroads into management areas have been made by legislation, collective bargaining, and arbitration.

In principle, the supervisor is best advised to function on the premise that the parties have written a contract as an instrument containing specific and limited restrictions on the functions that management would otherwise be free to exercise if there were no labor contract. And, to whatever extent it has not, management continues to have all those rights that it customarily possesses and did not surrender on the collective bargaining process. Therefore, supervisors are best advised to subscribe to the principle that their management continues to possess the residue of all rights not bargained away. However, he must also be urged to recognize that the union is also a party to the labor agreement. To the extent that the company has agreed to compromise or restrict its managerial discretions, he must realize that such matters are no longer within the province of his authority or control. He is urged to accept the premise that the union also has the right to enjoy the contract benefits and privileges obtained in negotiations with the employer and that matters falling within this area are beyond his authority to alter, modify, or reduce in any respect.

The Supreme Court of the United States has indicated that in the absence of a contractual provision limiting or prohibiting his right, an employer may legally discharge an employee for any or no cause, subject only to valid state or federal laws imposing limitations on him. In the case of *United Steelworkers of America v. Warrior & Gulf Navigation Co.,* the Court stated:

> Collective bargaining agreements regulate or restrict the exercise of management functions; they do not oust management from the performance of them. Management hires and fires, pays and promotes, supervises and plans. All these are part of its functions, and absent a collective bargaining agreement, it may be exercised freely except as limited by published law and by the willingness of employees to work under the particular, unilaterally imposed conditions....[4]

Actually, the right of an employer to discharge without just cause was a creature of the common law of the nineteenth century. One of the basic purposes of a collective bargaining agreement, at least for the union organization that negotiates it, is to modify this power and require the employer to deal justly with all employees when taking disciplinary or discharge action.

The National Labor Relations Act, the Taft Act, the Fair Employment Practices Act, the veterans' reemployment provisions of the Selective Service Act, and other statutes have all circumscribed the right of employers and the scope of their powers to discharge without just cause. The adoption of a collective bargaining agreement by an employer nearly always results in a further narrowing of his discharge powers, irrespective of whether it spells out such restrictions in detail.

The parties to labor agreements appear to deal with the problem of management's power to discipline and discharge in one or more of three ways.

First, they may adopt a generalized management protection clause that provides an outline and review of the various prerogatives reserved to the employer. Typical of such a clause is one that reads:

> Recognition of Management: The Management has the responsibility to direct the operations of the Company and to determine the number and location of its plant or plants and departments therein; the products to be manufactured; the methods, processes, and means of manufacturing; the sources, materials, and supplies; and the disposition of products. The Company also has the right to discipline or discharge any employee for just cause and to transfer and lay off because of lack of work or for

other legitimate reasons, provided that none of these functions of the Management shall be exercised so as to abrogate or nullify any specific provision of this Contract. Any dispute arising therefrom shall be taken up and adjusted under the regular grievance procedure.

Second, employers and unions may work out contractual terms relating specifically to discharge and disciplinary cases. The following is a standard example:

> Any employee who has been disciplined by a layoff or a discharge may request the presence of the Shop Steward of his area to discuss the case with him before he is required to leave the plant. The Shop Steward will be called promptly.
>
> Any employee who is removed from his work and taken to an office for interview may, if he so desires, call the Shop Steward to be present with him during the interview. The Shop Steward, however, will be present only as a witness for the employee, and may negotiate on the matter only after the employee has a grievance as a result of the interview.
>
> It is important that complaints regarding unjust or discriminatory layoffs or discharges be handled promptly according to the grievance procedure.
>
> Grievances must be filed within forty-eight (48) hours of the layoff or discharge, and the Company will review and render a decision on the case within five (5) working days of its receipt.
>
> If the employee is not found to be unjustly disciplined by layoff or discharge, such layoff or discharge shall be absolute as of the date of such disciplinary action.
>
> If, after the decision of Management, the case is not appealed by the Shop Committee within five (5) working days, the matter will be considered closed.

The third form of contractual provision concerns primarily the employer's right to maintain order and efficiency through shop rules or similar devices. A typical clause states:

> The rules and regulations of the Company shall continue in full force and effect, and the Company shall have the right to amend such rules and regulations and to make further rules and regulations, provided they are not contrary to the terms of this Agreement and provided that a copy of any amendments or further rules and regulations shall be submitted to the Chairman of the Bargaining Committee twenty-four (24) hours before posting, except in case of emergency.

A 1980 Bureau of National Affairs study showed that 82 percent of 400 contracts contained a general statement relative to the grounds for discharge, such as just cause. A total of 21 percent contained an itemization of company rules. Failure to meet work standards was a basis for dismissal in 18 percent of this sampling, a contract violation committed by an employee in 30 percent, and an employee's unauthorized absence — most frequently of three to five days or an "excessive" number of times — in 20 percent.

An examination of these contracts revealed that the parties had agreed on certain procedures for management to follow when it was either contemplating or actually instituting a discharge action. A warning was required before discharge in 7 percent of the cases. The employer was obliged to issue a notice to the employee of the contemplated action in 25 percent of the agreements, with notice to the union required either preceding or following the dismissal in 32 percent of the 400 contracts. In 7 percent, the employee had to have previously been suspended before discharge could be instituted. Union participation in the procedure was required in 6 percent of the contracts, and 9 percent provided for the company to hold hearings or discussions with the employee and/or the union before discharge could be imposed.

Another aspect analyzed was the appeals and grievance machinery designed for the specific purpose of handling discharge cases: special procedure appeared in 8 percent of the agreements. Some contracts stipulated the period within which the discharged employee-grievant and/or the union was required to file a complaint contesting the action. The time limit of one to three days appeared in 23 percent, with 31 percent permitting four to seven days and another 7 percent providing for eight days or more.

Many of these labor agreements made some provision for the handling of cases of discharged employees who were later reinstated. A general statement dealing with this subject appeared in 53 percent of the contracts; 27 percent provided for reinstatement with full back pay and another 7 percent with only limited back pay; and 53 percent allowed for reinstatement at the discretion of an arbitrator.

Grounds for dismissal were detailed more frequently in manufacturing than in nonmanufacturing contracts — 62 percent versus 43. The causes most often specified were violation of the contract, violation of company rules, incompetence or failure to meet work standards, intoxication, dishonesty or theft, unauthorized or excessive absence, insubordination, and misconduct.

Other grounds that were stated, but much less frequently, included wage garnishments, immoral conduct, narcotics trafficking (maritime industry), bribe taking, and failure to obey safety rules (construction).

An interesting development that may represent a growing trend involves the contractual statute of limitations under which past offenses are wiped off the disciplinary record book after a specified period. Such a clause appeared in 17 percent of the agreements—19 percent of the manufacturing and 13 percent of the nonmanufacturing.

Although much less frequently found, there are labor agreements that prohibit arbitration review of discipline and discharge actions taken by the employer. These are voluntary issues for collective bargaining, according to an interesting legal separation articulated in a 1958 Supreme Court decision.[5] In it, the Court recognized three distinct categories of bargaining proposals and set down three types of rules regarding them.

Mandatory topics. Under the Labor Management Relations Act (LMRA), section 8 (d), both parties are required to negotiate in good faith with respect to wages, hours, and other conditions of employment. The party submitting such proposals may insist on their inclusion in any contract executed, and the other party is compelled to bargain on them. In this area, bargaining may proceed to an impasse.

Voluntary topics. Either party may place such topics on the table, hoping for voluntary bargaining and ultimate agreement. However, the receiving party cannot be required either to negotiate on them or to agree on their inclusion in any contract executed. If the advancing party demands their inclusion—in other words, insists on bargaining to an impasse—this constitutes a violation of its bargaining duty under the act.

Illegal topics. Subjects forbidden under the LMRA would include such things as proposals for a closed shop. Neither party can insist that the other bargain on these topics, and they are improper if later included in the agreement even with the other party's consent.

Where does collective bargaining on discipline and discharge fit into this legal picture? The answer is that an employer must be willing to discuss the issues of discharge and discipline with employees or their representatives. However, the National Labor Relations Board (NLRB) has ruled that an employer did not violate his bargaining duty when he insisted on excluding these issues from the arbitration process. In this significant holding, the Board found that the company was quite willing to discuss its challenged discharge and discipline actions all through the grievance procedure; it insisted only upon not arbitrating them. The employer's right to this position was supported by the Board.[6]

Contractual Limitations

It seems to be a well-established rule of contract administration as handed down in the great majority of arbitral opinions that an employer does not have an unrestricted right to discipline, even though the collective bargaining agreement does not expressly and specifically limit it.

In other words, the mere presence of a labor agreement tends to require the employer to act only for cause. The reasoning is that a fundamental purpose of the agreement is to provide the workers with some form of job security. To allow an employer to exercise, solely, his own discretion in determining the justness of his discipline and discharge actions would render this premise null.

A number of cases from respectable arbitral authority support this conclusion. For example, though dealing with a labor agreement that did not expressly qualify the company's disciplinary power with a just cause requirement, Arbitrator Walter E. Boles evaluated the propriety of the employer's discharge action according to this standard. He founded his argument on the premise that a just cause basis for discipline is implied in an agreement in the absence of a clear proviso to the contrary. In this holding, the arbiter referred to another decision of his, an unpublished one that involved the Southwestern Bell Telephone Company and the Communications Workers of America, and then stated:

> The arbitrator is fully aware that the Contract between these parties does not contain the conventional "just" or "proper" cause language in connection with disciplinary matters.
>
> But certain realities must be recognized.... The first "reality" in the situation is that the Arbitrator must consider this "issue" on the same basis he would use if the Contract provided for "discharge for just cause." Any other approach simply is not realistic [today] ... (when the bulk of the 100,000 collective bargaining agreements contain "just cause" or make "just cause" appraisals of disciplinary action, they should so indicate in their writing).[7]

Most managements want and attempt to interpret and administer the labor agreement as though it contained the only limitations on their absolute right to manage the enterprise as they see fit. Under this concept, they are wont to argue that the union's claims must fall unless it can point to a specific contractual provision on which its action is based.

On the other hand, most arbitrators concur in the view that there are too many unforeseeable contingencies for a contract to constitute the sole definition of the privileges accorded to the union and the employees during its term; moreover, with a document only 25 to 75 pages long, there may be inadvertent or even deliberate omissions. The parties may attempt to regulate all aspects of their complicated relationship from the most crucial to the most minor by giving as extensive and comprehensive specifications as they can formulate. But this is not often possible or even practicable because of the compulsion to reach agreement and the breadth of the matters covered as well as the need for a fairly concise and readable instrument. The product of negotiations—the written document—is, in the words of the late Harry Shulman, "a compilation of diverse provisions; some provide objective criteria almost automatically applicable; some provide more or less specific standards which require reason and judgment in their application; and some do little more than leave problems to future considerations with an expression of hope and good faith."

An interesting and peculiar aspect of discipline and discharge controversies is that the parties to labor agreements appear to be much less articulate in drafting the clauses governing such matters than they commonly are on almost all other potential problems. This may be because of the sensitivity of the subject to both sides and their inability or unwillingness to cope with it comprehensively. Employers may refrain from giving it full language coverage in the hope of retaining greater latitude in their decisions. Unions may be motivated by the feeling that the less said explicitly about the subject, the greater will be the question in an arbitrator's mind as to the scope of management's power to act. Although these are only speculations, one thing is certain: The majority of collective bargaining agreements speak far less concretely on discipline and discharge problems than on most other contractual points.

Past Practice

Gaps left in a contract may be filled in by reference to the practices of the particular industry and of the various shops covered by the agreement. An example of the limitations that such precedents can impose on management's power to discharge or discipline is found in a decision by Arbitrator John W. May. The dispute involved a contract that contained no provision relating to the discharge of employees. Over the objections of the company, a union representative reported off from work for union business. Upon his return, the company had a replacement for him. Almost immediately thereafter, the company discharged the union official, alleging that he had caused a strike to take place because he was provoked by the company's action in replacing him. When the union's grievance was argued before the arbitrator, the employer contended that no law or agreement prohibited the company from dismissing an employee. The only mention of discharge in the contract was contained within the union's security provisions dealing with employees' failure to pay union dues. The arbitrator's comments relative to the employer's position and the weight of past practice in the absence of contractual language are worthy of review:

Under the conditions of no Contract provision to the contrary the Company arrogates [to] itself the right to discharge with or without reason. This is legalism in its most abused form. There is no reason why if the Contract is silent it could not then be interpreted in exactly the reverse form so that the Company would be unable to discharge an employee for any reason. The silence of the Contract could be used in such a way that all discharges are legal except those violative of Federal or State statute. The legal profession has long since recognized that not all incidents are covered by statutory enactment and jurists have developed the law of equity to deal with such cases. An arbitration proceeding is more like equity than statutory law proceedings. We are here lacking a rule of law due to its absence in the Contract and equity must, therefore, prevail.

Again reliance must be had [on] past practice, since rules of conduct are lacking in the Agreement. Mr. Edward Bamford testified the Company was responsible in its dealings with its employees and had few discharges in its history, not more than 15 in 30 years of operation. Further, there was good cause underlying these dismissals, in most cases dishonesty. Herein is the pattern over the past 30 years of discharge for just cause. In the case of X_____, therefore, just cause must also be shown. This cannot be construed as writing in or amending the Contract when a practice has existed for 30 years and serves as a basis for negotiation and agreement.[8]

A labor agreement contained a statement in the management's rights clause that the employer retained the sole right to discharge. Arbitrator R.H. Morvant held that, though rights may be reserved in this way, this did not mean they were unrestricted. He reasoned that they were expressly qualified by two other provisions of the contract, which provided for loss of seniority and vacation rights upon discharge "for cause" and thus clearly established that management's right was intended to be limited to discharge for cause. It was the employer's argument that the term "for cause" could not be interpreted to mean just or good cause, and he therefore might discharge for any reason without protest. Morvant rejected this contention on the ground that it annuls the basic principles of all labor-management agreements. He made the following comments on this point:

The labor-management agreement reduces to writing the rights of the individual worker and protects those rights against any arbitrary or unfair action on the part of representatives of the company. To agree with the Company that "cause" in this instant case means "any reason" would make meaningless all the rights of the individual worker. If the Company can discharge and not be subject to protest for such unilateral action, it is conceivable that the Company could abrogate all of the provisions of the Agreement, including the wage rates, simply by discharging any employee who dared to protest. Consequently, we must interpret the term "discharge for cause" as denoting a fair and legitimate reason for termination, since such action cuts brutally across the economic life of the person involved.[9]

Other decisions reflect the arbitral viewpoint that each collective bargaining agreement tacitly assumes an employer shall not arbitrarily exercise his power of discharge. Accordingly, it has been held that an employer was not free to act without just cause despite the absence of a contract clause stating this.[10] In a dispute at the Atwater Manufacturing Company, for example, the company claimed unlimited discharge powers under a collective bargaining agreement that did not expressly restrict them. A board of three arbitrators rejected this view on the ground that, if the company could discharge without cause, it could also lay off without cause. Further, it could recall, transfer, or promote in violation of seniority provisions simply by invoking its claimed right to discharge. They expressed their rationale in these words:

> A collective bargaining agreement is a comprehensive instrument by virtue of which the parties agree to recognize respective rights. No agreement covers all questions which might arise under its terms and because of this the parties included a grievance procedure and its arbitration to resolve questions as to the meaning of the agreement and its application. However, basic to every agreement must be a quality of consistency and logic. Obviously, parties will not by agreement bind themselves to provisions which are contradictory and meaningless. Thus, when one of the parties claims a right which the explicit terms of the agreement either modify or abolish, the claimed right will need strong argument to stand.
>
> In the instant case the Company claims an unlimited right to discharge. The basis of its claim is that the Agreement does not state that the Company does not have the right. The fact is, however, that in the Agreement both the Company and the Union have agreed on definite employee rights, which rights would be meaingless if they did not necessarily imply a severe modification of the Company's right to discharge.
>
> Thus, the explicit terms of the Agreement, by establishing rights which are wholly inconsistent with the claims of the Company, must logically be considered to have modified any claimed rights which are not there expressed and which are inconsistent with the explicit terms of the Agreement.[11]

All the above decisions have a common thread of reasoning running through them: An employer's powers of discharge are curtailed with the birth of the written labor document. Such limitations are an implied term of the contract, created by the necessity for preserving harmony among the contract's component parts.

The question may also arise whether a company may discipline for a lesser degree of an offense than the contract stipulates. For example, does the use of the term "gross negligence" in a labor agreement prohibit an employer from discharging an employee for ordinary negligence? That was one of the issues facing James V. Altieri in settling a dispute between the Brewer Dry Dock Company and the Brewer Dry Dock Employees Association, Inc. The agreement stated that the employer retained the right to "discipline an employee for violation of rules or other proper cause," and "proper cause" might be "drunkenness or insubordination, or habitual taking of days off, or gross negligence, or theft from fellow employees or from the company, or fighting or gambling on company property." Although the union conceded that employees could properly be found guilty of ordinary negligence, the company could not invoke the discharge clause because it defined only gross negligence as proper cause for disciplinary action, so that by implication ordinary negligence was excluded. The arbiter disagreed. He felt that the examples of proper cause listed in the contract were not intended to be complete or exclusive but illustrative only, so as to eliminate from dispute the question of whether the conduct described warranted disciplinary action.[12]

Some companies have discovered, probably much to their chagrin, that individual employee contract rights may govern their discharge decisions after an existing collective bargaining agreement has expired. Such has been the holding by both arbitrators and courts. According to one court's finding, the terms and conditions of a collective bargaining agreement provide rights that establish a standard for the individual employment contract embracing each worker that comes into operation upon the expiration of the collective bargaining instrument.[13]

Court decisions take into account any actions of the employer during the period between the expiration of the agreement and the commencement of the negotiated instrument that follows it. The investigation traces the character of the interim relationship between the parties to determine whether they intended to conduct it in keeping with terms that had outlived the prior agreement.

Where an employer has taken steps to establish new conditions governing the relationship in the interim period, the courts have ruled differently. For example, an employee was laid off during the term of a contract that contained a seniority clause entitling him to reinstatement. Before his reinstatement, the contract expired. The court held that labor agreements do not "extend rights created and arising under the contract beyond its life, when it has been terminated in accordance with its provisions," and that the "rights of the parties to work under the contract persist during [and] end with its term."[14]

When the contract expired, the company had posted rules that defined the employment relationships with the workers for the interim period during which no collective bargaining agreement existed. Subsequently, it entered into a labor agreement with the union. In this instance, neither the posted rules nor the later negotiated instrument provided the laid-off employee protection of his seniority rights. Therefore, no implied individual contract could be presumed that maintained the stipulations in the expired agreement: The employees' acceptance of the company-established rules and the later negotiated instrument produced express contracts that governed the relationships during both these periods.

Arbitral opinion has held that individual employment contracts arise by implication where a collective bargaining agreement has expired and the union and the employer have failed to sign a new contract. The rationale behind this stand closely follows the reasoning in court decisions on such cases. In one dispute, the employer had not notified the employees of the terms under which they would continue to work — that is, the terms of the individual contract that would prevail — after the previously negotiated agreement had expired. The arbiter ruled that the provisions and exclusions of the collective instrument were still applicable to the people it had covered and thus governed the individual employer-employee relationship. The expired agreement had contained no specification of mandatory retirement age; accordingly, the company was held not to have just cause to discharge an employee on the ground that he had reached 65.[15]

Through a range of cases, then, arbitral and court opinion has considered management's prerogatives — whether expressed in the contract or implied as residual rights — to be qualified by the necessity that they be fair and reasonable rather than capricious or arbitrary. A company's inherent right to set and maintain workable standards of behavior for employees is counterbalanced by the presumption that it will exercise its authority and judgment equitably.

Establishment of Rules

Under its general rights article, management usually reserves the right to establish rules and procedures governing the conduct of its employees. The typical clause of this kind states that management may issue and promulgate such directives provided they are reasonable and do not establish conditions that may constitute a violation of the contract. This is commonly the limit of the language. However, a minority of labor agreements have actually outlined the specific rules, either including them among the contractual provisions that have been negotiated and agreed on or specifying that they will be unilaterally established by the employer as a function of the rights reserved to management. An even smaller number of labor agreements contain both the actual rules and regulations agreed on and the steps to be taken, including the penalties to be imposed in the event of infractions. The existence of some rules is essential to the orderly operation of any enterprise. A company is analogous to a small society. Just as the whole of society requires laws for its own well-being and for the protection of its citizens, so does the firm need rules and regulations aimed at furthering its interests and insuring the health, safety, and welfare of its employees. Since the primary responsibility for the operation of the enterprise rests with the management, it must have the authority to establish reasonable rules and to discipline and discharge if it is to meet its obligations to the owners, stockholders, and employees.

The labor agreement normally outlines the essential negotiated terms and conditions of employment that will govern the relationship of the parties for a prescribed period. The residual rights theory holds that all powers not limited or denied to a company by a contractual provision are reserved to management. It is not unheard of for a labor agreement to impose some restriction on the employer's right to issue rules and regulations, but this is very rare. In the absence of such a provision, the parties are generally assumed to have concurred that the employer is to deal with disciplinary matters and will do so reasonably and with sound discretion. The reserved rights theory constitutes a well-established and widely applied principle in interpretations of collective bargaining agreements and is supported by the overwhelming weight of respected arbitral opinion.

Test of Applicability

Most rules are promulgated by employers to produce orderly employee behavior that will result in an efficient and productive operation. Therefore, they are primarily anticipatory, intended to head off problems before they occur. However, some rules develop to cover situations the employer had not foreseen. Occasionally these are prompted by the improper behavioral stance of a small group of employees. Unions have been known to challenge the reasonableness of such a restriction on the contention that it was discriminatory—that a rule designed to prevent abuses by a comparatively small percentage of employees is unfair to the properly behaving majority.

Managements have always found that most employees are

conscientious and honest and are quite willing to comply with any reasonable rules made necessary by the employment relationship. Despite this fact, an employer is not prohibited from imposing a general requirement on even those workers who might not be tempted to behave improperly without it. Certainly it should not be necessary, and arbitrators so hold, for an industrial situation to become unmanageable because of widespread employee misconduct before the company may take reasonable steps to curtail it. The essence of every shop rule and disciplinary regulation is general and uniform applicability.

Test of Sufficient Publicizing

In society at large, ignorance of the law generally constitutes no excuse. The citizen who alleges ignorance to defend his violation of a given law is seldom excused by law-enforcement people. A somewhat different condition exists in industrial society: arbitrators have customarily held that an employee cannot be expected to comply with rules and regulations he does not know.

Rarely have arbiters upheld a management's attempt to discipline an employee for violating a rule that was not published or adequately promulgated. The employee's ignorance of it constitutes a sustainable defense if he can establish that he could not have known it. This is why some employers have chosen to enumerate their factory rules and regulations fully and prominently within the covers of the labor document. Still others publish them in an employee handbook, which, in addition, generally outlines other conditions or benefits in the employment relationship. The majority seem to prefer to use bulletin boards scattered throughout the operating facility. In any case, a management will find it extremely difficult to have a disciplinary action sustained by an arbitrator unless it can establish that it has taken steps to communicate its rules effectively.

Furthermore, it is usually advisable not to impose penalties for the infraction of a rule instantly following its publication. Most employers have found it better to issue the rule, advise employees of the date it will go into effect (perhaps one week later), and state that violations occurring thereafter will result in disciplinary penalties. This alerts the employees to management's position and enables them to make any necessary preparations for compliance with the rule.

Review and Consent by the Union

It is usually a good procedure for the employer to discuss new or revised plant rules with union officers before communicating them to the employees. This is merely a courtesy under a labor agreement that does not impose a contractual obligation on the employer to inform the union before issuing rules. On the other hand, advance communication may be necessary where there is a contractual provision on the subject.

For example, the McCord Corporation unilaterally instituted a rule requiring employees to clock in and out at lunch time for the purpose, it maintained, of improving administrative control. The union contested this action on the ground that the company was contractually prohibited from instituting what the union described as a new rule without first consulting it and getting its consent. The employer contended that such advance discussions were only a matter of business courtesy. The arbitrator did not wholly concur with either view. He held that the contract gave the employer the right to institute plant rules covering employee conduct so long as they did not violate the terms of the contract and were not used to discriminate against employees because of union membership. However, a supplemental agreement specifically excluding plant rules from the collective bargaining instrument obliged the employer to discuss new rules with the union—though not to obtain its consent— before putting them into effect. Thus the union should have been advised of the rule in advance.[16]

In another case, the United Baking Company unilaterally drew up a complete set of plant and work rules. Although some of the posted rules fell into areas in which the company might act on its own, others involved wages, hours, and working conditions about which the contract required it to bargain with the union. So finding, the arbitrator ruled that he had no alternative under the agreement but to declare that the entire set of rules was invalid.[17]

Revisions in Rules

Arbitral opinion regarding revisions in existing rules is influenced by two factors. The first is the conditions of employment that the rule change will encompass. Thus a revision that directly affects the size of work crews, the amount of pay, or another question basic to the employment relationship is accepted less often than one dealing with a peripheral matter such as safety rules, work clothing, or a procedure intended to improve operating efficiency. The second factor is the weight of past practice. Unions commonly raise past practice as a defense when management attempts to impose a rule change that will reduce a benefit or condition previously enjoyed by the employees.

However, in the majority of instances, if the revision does not negatively affect the negotiable areas expressly addressed in the contract, most arbitrators will allow it on the ground that management has the same reserved right to revise rules as it has to issue them.

In disputes in which the union uses past practice to counter an employer-established rule or a revision, the employer will typically parry with the reserved rights argument that it has the power to promulgate rules or change them. Any rule that threatens the negotiated security derived from existing wages, hours, and working conditions is particularly worrisome to the union and usually meets with vigorous resistance from it.

One such provocative area involves the production standards that employees are expected to satisfy in the performance of their tasks. When these are the subject of controversy, it is more common for the employer than the union to rely on past practice to support its position. For example, the National Lead Company of Ohio had a long-standing labor agreement under which it had established production quotas for employees in the machining unit. During the term of the agreement, it instituted time and motion studies and other scientific tests looking toward a revision of the standards. When the tests were completed, employees were notified of new quotas and the amount of production to be expected from each worker. No incentive system was involved here; employees were paid an hourly rate, and each was assigned a certain number of pieces or parts to produce during each shift of work, failing which he could be liable to a disciplinary procedure. The union challenged the employer's right to set such standards.

There was no question before the arbitrator as to whether the standards were fair or unfair. The contract recognized management's right to adopt and enforce reasonable rules and regulations for efficient operations, and the employer was supported by the weight of past practice in that previous production quotas had been unilaterally established without complaint from the union. Arbitrator Carl R. Schedler therefore ruled that the employer had the right to set new standards unilaterally and to impose disciplinary penalties for failure or refusal to meet the quotas.[18]

It is not uncommon for a labor agreement to contain no provision that specifically authorizes or prohibits the establishment of production standards, though in this even other clauses may implicitly recognize this right. A statement in the contract that the management of the plant, and the direction of the workforce, is vested exclusively in the company, for example, would constitute such an acknowledgment in the view of most arbitrators, provided that the company did not invoke this implied right for the purpose of circumventing any other contractual provision.

A word of caution is in order here regarding rules governing production standards. It is inadvisable for quotas to be set on an individual employee basis. Arbitrators have held that management can set a standard of proper production only for a *job*. They have also held that where an employee was producing at a rate considered satisfactory for other employees, although perhaps not equal to his previous better effort, the employer was wrong in imposing a disciplinary penalty on him.[19]

Statutory Limitations

In its administration of the Labor Management Relations Act, the National Labor Relations Board has distinguished between "unlawful" employee activities, which are expressly barred by the unfair practices provisions of the LMRA, and "unprotected" activities, which are not expressly banned. The Board has held that employees engaging in concerted action that is found to be unprotected forfeit their rights under the LMRA and thus cannot successfully obtain reinstatement through the NLRB if they are discharged for such action.[20]

One court has said that an employee "may be discharged . . . for a good reason, a poor reason, or no reason at all, so long as the terms of the LMRA statute are not violated."[21]

Stating this opinion even more specifically, the United States Supreme Court has said that the act "permits a discharge for any reason other than union activity or agitation for collective bargaining."[22]

Putting it another way, a third court has said, "The question is not whether the discharges were related or unrelated, or just or unjust, nor whether as disciplinary measures they were mild or drastic. These are matters to be determined by management." This court commented that the sole duty of the National Labor Relations Board was to determine whether the discharges had the purpose of discouraging or encouraging union membership or taking reprisals against employees for engaging in concerted activities protected under the law.[23]

Federal Laws

The most significant statutory limitation on management's right to discipline or discharge is section 8 (a)(3) of the Labor Management Relations Act, which makes it an unfair labor practice for an employer "by discriminating in regard to . . . tenure of employment to encourage or discourage membership in any labor organization." Further, section 8(a)(4) forbids a management "to discharge or otherwise discriminate against an employee because he has filed charges or given testimony under this Act." The Fair Labor Standards Act (FLSA) likewise protects employees who institute actions under the law or testify in proceedings. The question of whether a discharge was actually motivated by such a reason is determined by the same kinds of tests used to decide whether an employer was imposing a penalty for union activity.

Legislation not related to management-labor relations may contain special clauses bearing on employees' rights. For example, section 9(c) of the Universal Military Training and Service Act states that veterans restored to their former positions after honorable discharge from the armed forces cannot be discharged without cause within one year.

Another provision of the LMRA, section 8(a)(1), makes it unlawful for an employer to interfere with the right of employees to engage in concerted activities for the purpose of mutual aid or protection. It is significant to employers that the NLRB may consider a discharge to violate this provision even though there is no evidence of union activities and no proof of unlawful motivation on the employer's part. Management must be cautious in taking disciplinary action against any employee who appears to be the communicator of fellow workers' complaints regarding wages, hours, or working conditions. It is not necessary for an actual labor organization to be involved. The employee who acts as a spokesman for his peers, whether he is self-appointed or otherwise, is engaged in "concerted activity," which is protected under federal labor laws. Although the employer may not be required to actually negotiate with a group (or its spokesman) unless evidence is shown that it represents a majority of the employees in a unit appropriate for collective bargaining, he is prohibited under the law from discharging the members for their group activity.

Management's primary concern is that the enterprise function as efficiently as possible. In order to accomplish this objective, it must sometimes take disciplinary or discharge action against employees for insubordination, inefficiency, or troublemaking. In the light of the federal labor statutes protecting employees' rights to join or organize unions and to take part in other concerted actions with legitimate aims, the employer must be constantly on guard not to confuse unacceptable behavior on the job with pursuits that are sanctioned by the law. The dividing line between protected and unprotected activity is indistinct; a review of pertinent NLRB cases demonstrates that the decisions do not follow a hard and fast pattern. In other words, what the NLRB will consider indefensible union conduct and what it will find to be legitimate —

although perhaps overexuberant — concerted activity is not always predictable.

In all such disputes, it is the task of the National Labor Relations Board to determine whether the employer's motive in discharging the employee was to punish him for his union activity.

In addition to the unpredictability of any Board decision, another factor the employer must consider carefully is that a ruling against its discharge action can prove very expensive. Besides the cost of mounting a defense before the NLRB, the company may also have to assume the burden of a large back pay award. Such disputes do not move speedily through the Board's slow machinery; they may take many months and even years. If the Board ultimately finds in the employee's favor, back pay will have grown large during this time. Naturally, the employee is supposed to seek other employment actively. But even if he succeeds in locating other work, the company may still have to make up the difference between his pay on the new job and what he would have received if he had not been discharged.

Certain employee activities may result in the removal of the limitations that the LMRA imposes on the employer's rights to discipline or discharge. This occurs in situations where employees have engaged in conduct that the act either specifies to be unlawful, such as a secondary boycott, or merely does not protect, such as an employee strike in violation of a no-strike clause under a labor agreement.

Discrimination Cases

A number of factors are always considered and reviewed by the National Labor Relations Board when it is conducting its investigation to determine whether a discharge was illegal under federal labor laws. It will be seeking answers to a number of questions; and if an employer who is involved in such a dispute answers them honestly to himself, he may be able to judge how successful he will be in his dealings with the Board:

1. What is the company's attitude toward unions generally? What is its attitude toward the union involved in the dispute?

2. What is its attitude toward the individual who has been discharged? Was it aware that the employee was a union member, advocate, or officer? What was the employer's relationship with the individual when he was functioning in a representative capacity?

3. Was a reason for discharge given to the employee when the action was taken? Was the same reason given at that time as is now provided?

4. What is the company's actual reason for discharging the employee? Does the evidence suggest some other motive could have been involved? Was the reason given in writing? If it was given orally, can the employer substantiate precisely what was said?

5. Has the company applied the same penalty to other workers who were guilty of the same offense? Has the rule been enforced consistently?

6. Was the rule communicated fully to the employees, and did it establish a clear policy regarding discharge actions?

If the employer's rule has not been enforced uniformly, the odds are against his being able to show that any discharge was not discriminatory. His problems will be compounded if the rule has not been generally disseminated or has been newly promulgated. On the contrary, the Board has been known to uphold the discharge of a union president when it was shown that he had violated a rule applied equally and impartially to all employees. However, a discharge for stealing company gasoline was ruled discriminatory by the Board when it appeared that it was a common offense not usually penalized.

A discharge occurring shortly after an employee's participation in a union activity is always suspect. In such an instance, the Board will examine very carefully the reasons given by the employer. An example of this is a case where the company claimed there was less need for the work done by the laid-off employee. The employer's defense immediately fell.[24]

This does not mean that the timing of a discharge or layoff is proof of discrimination. Timing is only circumstantial evidence, which can be overcome by proof that the reasons given for the action are proper. A company that discharged a union official on the same day he openly distributed union authorization cards was able to have its action supported by showing that the discharge was based on the employee's failure to obey safety regulations and that the decision had been made at an earlier date.

Other circumstances are likely to be considered evidence that a discharge or layoff is discriminatory. These are particularly relevant if the employee is a union member or has led a concerted activity intended for the benefit of fellow workers. Here are some typical examples.

A management discharged several workers and at the same time increased the wages and improved the benefits of other employees in an attempt to defeat unionization.[25] The Board found evidence of discrimination in another case when employees were discharged without any prior warning that this penalty could result from the conduct alleged as the cause of the discharge.[26] The same finding was brought when a company imposed discharges despite a serious labor shortage.[27]

In another case, the Board considered the taint of discrimination present when management discharged employees who had refused to help the company fight union activity.[28] When a company retained nonunion workers and later filled the jobs of discharged union members by hiring new people, the Board found the employer's actions discriminatory.[29] And more than one case has shown that when an employer questions an employee regarding union membership, puts him under surveillance to determine whether he attends union meetings, and then in this contaminated atmosphere discharges him or lays him off, there are already two strikes against the company that is charged with discrimination.[30]

2. Basic Principles of Discipline

No attempt is going to be made here to cover all of the complex aspects of the application and administration of industrial discipline and discharge. It would take an entire volume to do justice to this subject.

All that will be covered here are a few of the more basic but primary principles which all too often escape the realization or the appreciation of management supervisory representatives. Understanding these fundamental principles, when coupled with a particular institution's rules and regulations, practices and procedures, should enable a more correct administration, with fewer actions later overturned.

Purpose

The purpose of discipline is to correct improper conduct, not merely to punish for it. Therefore, in any given case, only the amount of punishment necessary to get an employee's attention and surely get the corrective message across to him, is the amount of penalty applied. The objectives of management in applying discipline are basically as follows: (a) enforce reasonable rules; (b) to help the employee help himself to be a better worker, to protect his job and thereby his family's security; (c) to save the company's investment, plus its training and replacement costs; (d) to protect the health and safety of all employees; (e) to protect the company's property and equipment; (f) to warn other employees that improper conduct will be punished, thereby (g) deterring other employees from similar misconduct on their part in the future; (h) to obtain a full day's work; and (i) to teach thereby a concept of self-discipline to all employees. Growing out of this is a means by which order is maintained, and limits are set for individual behavior which preserve the well-being of the entire group. The responsibility for all of this rests with the management, since only it can act — not the union, not the employees.

Ignorance of Law

In society at large, ignorance of the law generally constitutes no excuse for a particular behavior. The citizen who alleges ignorance to defend his violation of a given law is seldom excused by law-enforcement people. A somewhat different condition exists in industrial society where it has been customarily held that an employee cannot be expected to comply with rules and regulations he is not aware of.

Rarely has a management attempt to discipline an employee for violating a rule that was not published or adequately promulgated been upheld. The employee's ignorance of it constitutes a sustainable defense if he can establish that he could not have known of the alleged rule. This is why some employers have chosen to enumerate their factory rules and regulations fully and prominently within the covers of the labor document. Still others publish them in an employee handbook, while the majority seem to prefer to use bulletin boards scattered throughout the operating facility. In any case, a management will find it extremely difficult to have a disciplinary action sustained by an arbitrator unless it can be established that it has taken steps to communicate its rules effectively.

Just Cause

Most labor agreements contain a provision in the management rights article which states that the employer may "discipline or discharge employees for "cause" or "just cause" which must be met when discipline is meted out.

Very basically, it consists of three parts: (1) was an improper act, in fact, committed; (2) consequently, is the offense serious enough to warrant discipline; and (3) if so, is the penalty imposed appropriate to the offense.

The supervisor must justify each of these three parts. The union can protest and appeal any one or more of these parts, and an arbitrator reviews all three parts. The union may contest whether or not an improper act was actually committed and if it was, whether any discipline should be imposed based on the facts and circumstances; they can also grieve the penalty on the basis that it exceeds the amount of action necessary to correct the employee without being onerous or punitive.

These three parts, then, are those which shore up the foundation of "just cause."

Arbitrator Carroll R. Daugherty has developed seven criteria that he has set forth and applied in a number of published decisions on discipline cases. The stature of this arbiter makes these particular standards noteworthy. They are embroiled in seven questions.

> 1. Did the employee have foreknowledge that his conduct would be subject to discipline, including discharge? [This, of course, involves the "Ignorance of the Law" principle earlier enunciated.]
> 2. Was the rule he violated reasonably related to the safe, efficient, and orderly operation of the company's business?
> 3. Did the company make a reasonable effort before disciplining him to discover whether he in fact did violate this rule?
> 4. Was its investigation fair and objective?
> 5. Did it obtain substantial evidence that the employee was guilty of the offense with which he was charged?
> 6. Was its decision nondiscriminatory?
> 7. Was the degree of discipline given him reasonably related to the seriousness of his proven offense and/or his record with the company?[31]

Although a number of other arbitral opinions are available for review here, Daugherty's carefully reasoned standards are the most comprehensive, yet succinct. For an employer's discipline or discharge to be upheld, all seven questions must be answerable in the affirmative. If any one question evokes a negative response, the company's action will either fall or be amended. It should be noted that all of these seven criteria fall under the fundamental and general umbrella definition of just cause herein previously given.

Burden of Proof

It seems to be a well-established tenet of labor relations that the burden of proof in disputes over discipline or discharge must be carried by the party holding the affirmative of the issue — that is, the party who initiated the challenged action. The employer is therefore called on to establish the facts it asserts as the basis for having taken positive corrective action. The company must bear the burden of proving its action met the standards of just cause. The employee is innocent until proven guilty, and is presumed so.

In the grievance procedure, the employer should put forth the facts and evidence it holds in support of its action. Nothing of any relevance should be withheld.

If the case goes to arbitration, the company as the moving party here will undoubtedly be required to put on its case, in chief, before the union goes forward. Nothing should be withheld. On the other hand, nothing can be presented there in evidence against the employee, which has not been revealed and given to the union prior to the arbitration hearing. In fact, many contracts preclude the introduction of any matters not presented between the parties during the course of arguing the case within the steps of the grievance procedure.

The employee need not testify during the arbitration hearing. His waiver or refusal to do so will *not* raise any presumption as to his guilt or culpability. He need not prove his innocence — the employer, the moving party on discipline and discharge actions, must prove his guilt.

Was a crime committed? Was this the employee who committed the offense? Was he previously aware it would be deemed improper? Was corrective action merited? Was the amount of discipline imposed no harsher than should have been necessary to correct the problem?

The burden is not on the union to disprove the employer's action. The burden is on management to prove its decision was just and necessary.

Five Types of Industrial Offenses

There are basically only five different types of industrial offenses, and all of the specific violations of rules and regulations can be divided among, and assigned to, one of these five families.

1. A violation of the contract. In this category one will generally find offenses like: refusal to work overtime if otherwise mandated by the labor agreement; refusal to accept a work assignment or a transfer to another job; or engaging in a work stoppage or other action in contravention of the no-strike clause.

2. A violation of a plant rule. In this family of offenses one will generally find disputes involving violations of safety rules; carrying firearms; being under influence of alcohol or drugs; smoking; sleeping; etc.

3. Engaging in misconduct on plant premises and which is illegal in the community. Examples of this type of offense would be stealing, rape, molesting other employees, fighting and assault, and various manifestations of moral turpitude.

4. Engaging in misconduct on plant premises and which is not illegal in the community, but which does affect the employee's relationship with the company. Numbered among this type of offense would be those of horseplay, littering, neglect or abuse of tools and equipment, gambling, etc.

5. Engaging in misconduct off plant premises, which may affect the employee's job, his fellow employees', supervisor's, or the company's good will or reputation. There are many examples of this: an employee confronts and attacks his supervisor, off-plant, perhaps many miles away from the workplace. This is nevertheless misconduct which warrants disciplinary action, especially if such actions on his part resulted from carrying a work-related grievance off-premise. Another example could be an employee selling or giving formulae or trade secrets of his own employer's to one of its competitors. Or, perhaps a male employee engaged in off-premises conduct of an immoral or obscene nature (public indecency or attempted rape) with the consequence being that fellow female employees were fearful or refused to work with the offender any longer, on premises. Such instances as these, and a host of others, may constitute off-duty, off-premises conduct which justifies the employer in imposing some form of disciplinary or corrective action.

Reasonableness of Rules

The majority of management rights articles contain a provision which, in effect, says that the employer may "establish reasonable rules and regulations for employees to observe." The sense in which the term "reasonable" is used is what I will attempt to define here.

Rules which are reasonable are basically those which are reasonable in context; reasonable in their administration and enforcement; and reasonable in the penalties meted out for their violation.

The union may normally be free to grieve any one of these parts: the context of the rule, the manner of enforcement of the rule, and the penalties imposed thereupon.

A rule that is reasonable in context is one that has a bearing upon or a relatedness to the safe, efficient and orderly operation of the enterprise. Therefore, a rule prohibiting smoking in a potentially explosive or volatile work situation would certainly be deemed reasonable in context — whereas a rule of no-smoking in a foundry where there is already molten metal, sparks, fire, heat and smoke, could very probably be viewed as unreasonable in context.

A rule that is reasonable in enforcement and administration is one in which employees are treated relatively equally for infractions, so that misconduct by some is not overlooked while others are held to strict compliance. Therefore, a rule may be reasonable in context, but unreasonable in enforcement unless it is applied consistently, uniformly and regularly, between and among all employees.

A rule that is reasonable in the penalty imposed is one where the punishment fits the crime. For example, a rule against littering may be reasonable in its context — it may be uniformly enforced — but nevertheless unreasonable in terms of punishment if an employee is instantly fired, for a first offense, of inadvertently dropping a tiny piece of paper on the floor.

It is recognized that these are rather extreme examples, but deliberately so represented, to illustrate by dramatization the points being made.

Offers of Compromise

The purpose of the grievance procedure is to provide the parties with an orderly, regulated means for peacefully resolving their differences during the term of the agreement. For this process to operate effectively, the parties must each feel at liberty to suggest, and to offer, various remedies for such problems. They must feel they have the freedom to search for solutions which are accommodating to their respective interests. Such suggested remedies are put forth and analyzed, weighed and considered, sometimes to be accepted, other times to be declined or responded to with a counterproposal.

This is as it should be. And, to insure and preserve this grievance-bargaining freedom, many labor agreements contain a provision, usually found in the grievance or arbitration article, which basically states that such offers of compromise cannot be introduced to an arbitrator as evidence against the interests of the compromise-offering party.

However, even though such provision may not appear in the contract, arbitrators will typically disallow the introduction of any information of this type into the arbitral record.

The reasons for this customary holding are obvious. For example, the company discharges an employee and during the grievance procedure offers to reinstate him, less any back pay, with a 30-day suspension remaining on his record. The union declines, demanding full back pay as well, and no suspension whatsoever. The company refuses this union demand and the parties proceed to arbitration on the issue of the discharge.

The union in this case would be precluded from introducing to the arbiter the fact of the company offer to reduce its discharge action to a 30-day suspension. The arbiter would disallow this presentation. He must do so to preserve the parties' bargaining freedom in the grievance procedure. If he were to allow either party to introduce evidence of prior offers of compromise, and allow them to influence his decision, it would act to hinder or throttle the parties in their efforts to resolve problems by compromise and accommodation. Under those circumstances, each party would take stiff-legged, unbending positions throughout all steps of the grievance process, not offering in any way to compromise or otherwise seek solutions, since if they did so, such could be subsequently revealed as evidence against their own interests.

Therefore, supervisors should not worry about their efforts to resolve problems later being used against them. They won't be. That's what the grievance procedure is for. But, there is one additional word of advice in this connection.

Let us refer back to the discharge case just previously mentioned. After discharging the individual, which action was based upon certain facts, circumstances and evidence, a grievance results and the parties meet to discuss it. Previously, it was described that the company here offered to reduce its discharge action to a 30-day suspension from work without pay. Let us presume that such offer of compromise came because the union offered mitigating evidence and circumstances. The union feels it is sufficient to warrant removing all disciplinary action. Obviously, the company seems to feel it does affect its case, but not sufficiently to merit reinstatement in whole. So, the company offered to reduce its action and the union refused to accept. In the situation cited above, the employer withdrew its compromise offer, let its discharge action stand, and the parties proceeded to arbitration. In such a case as this one, or any others of a related nature, I would recommend a different company position.

Its discharge action was based upon certain facts, circumstances and evidence. The union comes along and produces mitigating circumstances and evidence, not known and/or considered by the company, when it decided to discharge. This information acts to somewhat compromise the viability of the company position. At this point, the company offers to reduce its action to a 30-day sentence without pay. I would urge that if this offer of compromise is declined by the union, that the employer unilaterally implement its offer of compromise — advise the employee of its revised action of a 30-day suspension without pay, and inform him when he is due back at work. In other words, don't withhold the compromise by basing its implementation upon union acceptance of it. If the total facts and evidence point toward that as a more appropriate disciplinary treatment, the arbitrator will undoubtedly think so too. So why let him do *to* you, what you can do *for* yourself. Additionally, all of the foregoing is material and facts which can be presented to the arbitrator as evidence of your reasonableness, willingness to compromise, and your determination to do what's right, because it's right, and not because you're ordered to.

Double Jeopardy

It is a well-established principle in labor-management relations that an employee cannot be punished twice for one offense. This is evidently an outgrowth of our constitutional prohibition against subjecting a person in a criminal proceeding to double jeopardy. The basis for the legal rule is the view that to try and then retry an accused for the same act would be an oppressive exercise of the power of the state against the individual. Our notions of fairness are offended by the thought.

This rule has been considered to have applicability to disciplinary proceedings in an industrial plant, for, as one commentator has said, double penalties "would be contrary to fundamental concepts of justice."[32]

Generally, the concept of double jeopardy is not found applicable in discharge cases involving a series of minor offenses when management has imposed corrective discipline properly.[33] Corrective discipline is progressive. Unless the employee's offense is so grave as to merit immediate discharge, the degree of punishment will be decided by how often he has erred before and how important the rule is that he has broken. A first offender guilty of a minor infraction of a rule is given a minor punishment, perhaps an oral warning or a written reprimand. If he breaches a similar or comparable rule on a second occasion within a reasonable time, a more serious penalty will usually be assessed. Further and harsher penalties may follow up to and include discharge. Each increasingly severe penalty is telling the worker that the gravity of his misconduct is increasing, and each affords him another opportunity to improve so that the terminal point of discharge may be avoided.

Each step probably constitutes a grievable situation, and every discipline imposed by the employer must stand the test of just cause. If the union challenges it unsuccessfully or lodges no grievance at all, the incident becomes a part of the employee's work record. Therefore, in an arbitration hearing on a dispute, the worker's prior disciplinary record is a highly relevant consideration. Thus, its introduction into the arbitration record does not expose the offending employee to any threat of double jeopardy.

Demotion — Withholding Benefits

Demotion as a form of discipline to correct improper employee behavior is an action to be discouraged. While it is true that a small majority of arbitrators disapprove of such action as a type of discipline, admittedly a good number would permit it unless it was clearly disallowed by the contract. I believe this is fallacious reasoning in the majority of such cases.

The opposite view is urged here. Demotion should only be considered and employed where the contract expressly provides for it. The single exception is one to be mentioned later herein. But, for the most part, demotion as a form of discipline should be shied away from.

Demotion does not correct an employee act of misconduct — it merely transfers it to a lower level, to another location, perhaps even to a different supervisor. It is a cop-out, an evasion, an escape hatch which, when used by the supervisor, enables him to avoid facing the employee's problem. Of course, what I'm talking about here are cases where the employee has violated some established plant rule or regulation which is designed to regulate his behavior, such rules as those covering absenteeism, tardiness, horseplay, smoking, drinking, loitering, littering, drugs, misuse of working time, and the like. Demotion is not an appropriate remedial action for correction of these types of misconduct.

As a matter of fact, it can be persuasively contended that to demote, unless specifically allowed by contract, denies the affected employee a contractual benefit. It probably affects his seniority ranking in some negative way. It probably results in a material reduction in his wage or salary — and such a penalty as that is ongoing, payday after payday, with no eventual terminal point. It in effect constitutes a form of withholding of a negotiated contract benefit. There is very little difference between that type of action and telling him he will get only eight holidays instead of ten (10) as contractually assured, or his insurance coverage will be unilaterally reduced below other employees' coverage, or everyone else will get the contractually provided rest periods but his are to be denied, etc. By demoting an employee, management can be imposing a penalty of indefinite duration. Its action can affect the seniority rights of not only the penalized worker but also others, who then become unintended victims. It can weaken the demoted employee's job security by making him more vulnerable to layoff. It may jeopardize his ability to obtain more meaningful and profitable positions in the future. It is too often a substitute for intestinal fortitude — an easy or at least less troublesome way out of a situation meriting discharge or another form of discipline. Further, it can result in the imposition of unequal penalties: One worker may be demoted three labor grades while another who is guilty of the same offense under similar circumstances may be demoted two or four.

The one exception, alluded to earlier, is that any demotion should be related to the employee's competence and qualifications for the job, not to breaches of plant rules, which call for discipline.

Moreover, if an employee has the ability to perform a job and is withholding it, this constitutes a condition that also is subject to correction through progressive discipline. The reason for the behavior is really irrelevant. Whether it arises from a misplaced sense of independence, work group pressures, or circumstances in his private life, there is no justification for it as long as any such conditions are within his control.

A case involving the Bethelehem Steel Company embodies this view. The arbitrator held that management's demotion of an employee was improper because his record indicated that he had the requisite ability for the job, stating that disciplinary action rather than demotion was proper remedy where substandard performance was found to be temporary.[34] The two significant facts are that the employee possessed ability and that he had demonstrated it. His failure to apply it to his task was merely temporary. The expectation was that he would regain his previous level of performance.

The arbitrator of another dispute held that the Boeing Company could use demotion when the employee was not capable of performing the work, but it was not entitled to demote where the evidence showed that errors were the result of negligence rather than inability.[35] Similarly, an arbitrator deciding a case involving the Republic Steel Corporation ruled that it could not use demotion as a form of discipline for occasional carelessness or failure to obey instructions on the job.[36]

All these decisions express the concept that as long as an employee is able and qualified to carry out his work, his failure to do so represents a fault that should be corrected by discipline rather than demotion.

Indefinite Suspension

If an employee is suspended from work without pay, as discipline for a work rules infraction, put a beginning and ending time and date on the suspension action. Don't leave it open-ended. There are several faults with handling it otherwise.

If you don't clearly define the duration of the suspension, the company is leaving its length to the discretion of the offender. What will you do if you order an insubordinate employee to go home, and not to come back until he is so disposed to follow the order. So, he takes you at your word, leaves, and six months later, or after any other period of time for that matter, comes back and says he's now inclined to follow your instruction. It sounds like he's more in command than you are.

Another fault with such an approach is of equal or greater consequence — such actions will not be supported by arbitral ruling.

The purpose of the discipline is to correct a given form of misconduct for the offender. In the occurrence described, a specific period of suspension should be given. The employer's presumption should be that the action taken has served its purpose when the worker returns following a suspension for a stipulated period. If the insubordinate or abusive employee continues his improper conduct upon his return or thereafter, he is subject to further disciplinary action for repeating the offense, up to and including discharge.

Workers should not be left to decide their own punishment. The responsibility for assessing the proper degree of penalty rests solely with the employer. He has failed to meet that responsibility unless he clearly declares the beginning and terminal dates of the discipline.

3. On-the-Job Reasons for Discipline

The activities for which employees are disciplined are far too numerous to be covered fully. To list them all and review some cases relevant to each would be a staggering undertaking, impossible to carry out within a single volume. What will be attempted here is a review of the kinds of situations that employers experience most commonly.

Mitigating Circumstances

When should exculpatory reasons mitigate the penalty of discharge? The Taft Broadcasting Company fired an employee for excessive absenteeism. The union argued that special circumstances, such as the employee's race, her relationship with other employees, and her home situation, had to be considered in the evaluation of just cause. The arbitrator, James V. Altieri, rejected this contention since the excessive absenteeism had admittedly occurred, it justified her termination regardless of the cause, and the penalty was not shown to be connected with any other punitive motive. He held that only if the primary issue were related to the mitigating circumstances would they be relevant.[37]

Arbitrator Thomas T. Purdom fashioned a unique remedy in resolving an absenteeism dispute. He first ruled that the company was justified in discharging an employee guilty of excessive absences during the two years preceding the present case. The employee had a health problem and had received doctor's orders to lose weight and stop smoking. It appeared that the employer had cooperated fully with him and the union regarding his health problem, but to no avail—his absenteeism continued.

A stipulation agreed to at the beginning of the hearing gave the arbiter great discretion, empowering him to reach a disposition that would have otherwise been impossible; without this latitude, he would have sustained the discharge and dismissed the grievance. The employee's work record before the past two years showed only four or five absences in 16 years. In view of this, the arbiter ruled that the worker could elect to take a leave of absence and return to work with full seniority if within

18 months he lost 150 pounds, stopped smoking, and obtained a doctor's certificate stating that he was able to take up his job again. His failure to meet these requirements within the allotted time would result in the permanent termination of his employment.[38]

Damage to or Loss of Materials

Employees are often disciplined for damaging or losing tools, equipment, or materials. For the action to be sustained, the damage or loss must be deemed to have been within the worker's control. Also, he must have been fully aware of his responsibilities with regard to the property.

The employee's action need not have been deliberate; it could have been negligent or careless. In either case, the burden of proof rests with the employer. Of course, if it is established that the damage or loss was intentional, a severer penalty will probably be upheld.

Negligent Acts

An employee failed to shut off a water valve at the right time, so that water spilled over and shorted out an electric motor. The resulting power failure caused a 50 percent reduction in operations for five hours. Turning off the water valve was a regular part of the job of this worker, who also had a previous record of discipline. The company imposed a two-week suspension for negligence, and the arbitrator upheld the action.[39]

An employee of Byerlite Co. of Koppers Co., Inc., was also held to have been properly discharged for negligence. While in charge of certain tanks that were being filled, he failed to cut off the intake in time to prevent excessive flow or overflow because he did not notice warning signs or take customary precautions.[40]

In an Ideal Cement Company case, a kiln burner closing down the kiln failed to take proper steps to reduce heat after the temperature in the kiln rose above the danger point. This resulted in serious damage to the equipment. The employee was discharged for gross negligence. The arbiter ruled that the evidence supported the charge, and in view of the fact that the employee had a record of two prior reprimands for sleeping on the job, he upheld the employer's action as having been taken for proper cause.[41]

Discharges have been reduced to temporary layoffs in instances where the employees have excellent work records or are on new jobs. These conditions were inapplicable in the cases just cited. The employees had ample familiarity with their tasks and had received discipline for related reasons previously.

Deliberate Acts

Where management takes action against employees for willful damage to company property, it bears a special obligation to prove its allegation. So the Publishers Association of New York City (the *New York Times*) discovered in a dispute with the New York Stereotypers Union.

A supervisor was observing an employee from some distance behind him. The man, visible only from the waist up, was making arm and body movements that appeared to be directed toward a piece of equipment in front of him. Several months before, he had been disciplined for willfully damaging company property. After watching him for a minute, the supervisor approached him, but on reaching the equipment he found him applying oil to the machine, a normal job responsibility. However, operating switches and fuses were found to be damaged, and the man was summarily discharged.

At the arbitration hearing, the foreman testified to what he had witnessed. The claim was that the worker had caused the damage to the machine, although it was admitted that the arm and body movements were akin to those of someone who was merely oiling it. The company's case, then, was based primarily on surmise. The union declined to present any evidence, arguing only that the company had failed to provide a prima facie case for its allegation. The arbiter agreed, and the man was reinstated with full back pay.[42]

In contrast to this decision is one that came out of a dispute at the General Electric Company. Arbitrator Donald A. Crawford rejected a union contention that the testimony of the company's eyewitness was not sufficiently convincing to support the decision handed down. Crawford commented:

> The Arbitrator cannot agree with the conclusion. H_____ was a very impressive witness. His location gave him an excellent view of what was going on below him including the Grievant's performance of his work. Nothing in the normal performances of the Grievant's duties would require him to strike the front right-hand side of the porcelain liner with a sharp blow of a hammer. Completely to the contrary, the fragile nature of the inner lining (glass) required that any work with a hammer, such as moving excess foam adhering to the liner or testing a "pimple," would be done carefully and gently—not by a sharp hammer blow. And H_____'s description of the blow was that of a sharp blow, not one

that could be mistaken for tapping excess foam away with his putty knife, or for an accidental dropping of his hammer, or for letting his arm fall to hit an already dented area.[43]

The difference betweeen the General Electric case and the *New York Times* matter is obvious. The *Times* foreman reported what he presumed he saw; the GE foreman reported what he witnessed firsthand from a clear vantage point.

At Quick Industries, Inc., sabotage and pranks had beset an assembly line for several weeks. The foreman had warned the assembly-line workers on various occasions that the trouble must stop, and the job superintendent had told them that the line would be shut down and they would be sent home if these acts continued. The incidents were causing a substantial disruption of production, loss of time, and consequently expense to the company. The discussions with the employees were of no avail. Finally, 12 of them were sent home an hour and a half before the end of their shift one day.

None of the facts just outlined was in dispute, and there was no question that the acts constituted just cause for discipline of the guilty. But before the test of just cause can be applied, adequate proof of the guilt of the person or persons involved must be established. This was not the case here. The arbiter was not unsympathetic to the gravity of the company's problem. But in his well-reasoned opinion, he stated that he believed he would be doing a disservice to the parties and would be violating a basic concept of American justice if he permitted a dismissal of this grievance.[44]

Justice William O. Douglas, referring to a Supreme Court decision, has written: "Guilt by association is a dangerous doctrine. It condemns one man for the unlawful conduct of another.... The almanac of liberty for the free world is filled with episodes where the means are plowed though the ends sought are worthy."[45] The American system of law comes from English common law as well as from statutes, and is based on a centuries-old concept that "it is better that ten guilty persons escape than that one innocent suffer."

These were the sentiments expressed by Arbitrator Jerome Gross in the above dispute. Their tenor was characteristic of him, and it can be found in the remarks of other jurists and teachers and in other citations of published labor arbitration reports.

Dishonesty

The term "dishonesty" is used here to mean misconduct that involves either money or property. It goes beyond misappropriation or theft in that it includes any conduct that tends to perpetrate a fraud on an employer resulting in financial loss. Some contracts actually define honesty and may even specify what would be considered dishonest acts. A list of abuses in this category would include taking or giving bribes, misusing company records, tampering with vending machines, padding expense reports, and using company funds for personal purposes. Falsifying work records or information on job applications, like theft, is troublesome and common enough to warrant separate treatment also; it will be taken up later.

Such dishonest acts as these, among others, have been established as providing just cause for discipline or discharge. The burden of proof rests with the employer, as always, and the punishment must be timely and befit the employee's work record. Because a charge of dishonesty reflects upon a person's character and standing in society at large, the evidence presented by the charging party, the employer, must be fully persuasive.

A company's failure to follow a long-established practice of notifying the union before firing an employee for dishonesty may be considered such a breach of procedure as to provoke an arbitrator to reinstate the worker. With some arbiters, the fact that the employee was caught red-handed may modify such an order. It has also been held that where the contract required the company to inform both the employee and the union within 72 hours of receiving evidence of the employee's dishonesty, the company could not postpone the notification while it gathered additional evidence.

Drinking

Almost all employers have a rule prohibiting employees from drinking on the job or reporting for work in an intoxicated condition, and probably no arbitrator would question management's right to enforce these prohibitions. But arbiters often rule that discharge is too severe a penalty, particularly for a first offense by an employee with a good work record and in the absence of convincing evidence that his condition prevented him from performing his job.[46]

Where the employee is in personal contact with the public at the time of the offense, a discharge for drinking is more likely to be upheld. This is also true when the job is such that drinking will endanger the safety of others, as in the case of truck driving.[47] In these instances arbitrators seem to apply a stricter standard.

Without doubt, it is critical that persons under the influence of alcohol be kept from behind a steering wheel. Therefore, a relatively low percentage of alcohol in the blood may be considered more dangerous in a driver than in a nondriver. For example, Sweden normally fines anyone found driving with an alcohol concentration exceeding 0.08 percent in the blood and sends those whose count surpasses 0.15 percent to jail. Norway punishes all who have a concentration exceeding 0.05 percent; the figure in Denmark is 0.10 percent. Many American states accept an alcohol concentration above 0.10 percent as prima facie proof of driving while under the influence of alcohol. Many authorities who assert that 0.10 is too high for normal purposes nonetheless urge an even lower figure in traffic cases, since they find that not only judgment but visual acuity and resistance to glare are affected long before visible signs of intoxication appear.

Claiming that an employee is intoxicated and proving it are two different things. As usual, and as it should be, the burden of proof rests with the company when it makes such an accusation. The tests that establish the degree of intoxication, however, are not always available to, or utilized by the employer. Therefore, some companies have taken to approaching the problem from a safer side.

Recognizing the complications of according with the burden-of-proof doctrine, an employer who firmly believes a worker is intoxicated may instead discipline or discharge him on the ground that he reported or is working "under the influence of intoxicants." To be "intoxicated" denotes loss of control of one's physical and mental faculties. To be "under the influence" denotes a lesser but appreciable effect on one's physical and mental powers because of alcoholic intake. In disputes over discipline based on this charge, the union often argues that what the employee does on his own time and while away from the plant is his business. This general statement is correct, but it has certain limitations. When the employee's off-duty activities affect his job performance, then the conduct becomes a matter with which the employer may be properly concerned, as we will see in some detail in the next chapter. Thus an employee who reports for work in a condition that does not allow him to do it properly is falling short of his obligations inherent in the employer-employee relationship.[48]

An especially cautious management that felt it had to discipline a worker for drinking might avoid even the phrase "under the influence" and rather base its action on a claim that he was in an "unfit" or "unsuitable condition" to perform his job. Indicators would be slurred speech, uncoordinated movements, staggering and a poor sense of balance, glazed eyes, rumpled clothes, an antagonistic manner, and so forth. A company using this approach trusts the arbitrator will deem signs like these to be evidence that the worker was temporarily incapacitated, without its needing to prove that such signs were the product of an inebriated state.

In the following case, the employer might have been well-advised to use one of these alternate strategies. Federal Services, Inc., discharged a plant guard for intoxication while on duty on the basis of witnesses' statements that the guard's lips were dry and that he burped. Although one observer "smelled no alcohol" and "didn't see him stagger," the guard was "a little unsteady on his feet and incoherent in his talk," and "something was obviously wrong" with him. All the company's witnesses testified that, in their best judgment, the grievant was intoxicated. However, it was the opinion of the arbiter that the facts they related were insufficient to justify their conclusion. He commented:

> Intoxication at work, particularly in a position as important and critical as that of a guard at an important defense installation, cannot be tolerated. But this does not lessen the requirement that the burden of proving a charge of this nature (intoxication) is on the Company, nor does it mean that in every case of suspected intoxication, the Company need impose the supreme penalty of discharge....
>
> The question of the Grievant's sobriety could readily have been documented had the Company sent the Grievant to a local hospital or other proper place for a sobriety test. By not doing this, in the face of the Grievant's and the Union's readiness to voluntarily submit the Grievant to such a test, the Company elected to base its case against the Grievant on the sound judgment of its own officials. And while they no doubt were entirely honest in their belief that the Grievant was intoxicated, other equally honest and competent observers held an opposite view.[49]

The grievant was reinstated in his job with back pay for all time lost. There is probably no recorded case that could provide a better example of why some employers have chosen to avoid the specific allegation that an employee is intoxicated.

Even when a company attempts to establish a charge of intoxication through a sobriety test, it may experience complications. In the following case, the company learned that it had not proved its allegation even though it had established that the worker's alcohol consumption exceeded generally accepted norms.

Kaiser Steel Corporation discharged for intoxication an employee whose blood test showed a 0.19 percent alcohol content. The sobriety scale used by the employer and many states sets the rating of 0.15 percent or more as conclusive evidence of intoxication. Arbitrator J.A.C. Grant overturned the discharge and ordered the grievant's reinstatement on these grounds: (1) the employee demonstrated no other clinical symptoms of intoxication, (2) medical authorities warn against accepting a specific rating as an index of intoxication without reference to other clinical symptoms, and (3) the employee was a heavy drinker and, according to medical opinion, could tolerate a higher concentration of alcohol in the blood than the average person without becoming intoxicated.

The medical literature referred to by this arbitrator includes the reprint files of the Alcohol Clinic of the Department of Psychiatry, the Medical School of the University of California at Los Angeles; 19 volumes of the *Quarterly Journal of Studies on Alcohol (QJSA),* published regularly since 1940; and a number of authoritative treatises such as Louis S. Goodman and Alfred Gilman's *The Pharmacological Basis of Therapeutics* (second edition, 1955). Arbitrator Grant's discussion is instructive for the extensive research it exhibits and thus warrants quoting at some length:

> Many studies have confirmed that the effects of alcohol on the central nervous system are more marked when the concentration in the blood is rising rather than falling. Similarly, when the alcohol concentration is increased and maintained following intoxication, the symptoms of intoxication disappear in from 4 to 10 hours at blood (alcohol) levels even higher than those at which they developed. In short, apparently the central nervous system acquires in time an ability to function more effectively at a given concentration of alcohol. Further evidence that a real tissue tolerance for alcohol develops is furnished by studies that have compared habitual heavy drinkers with moderate drinkers. Goodman and Gilman state, p. 106, that "The repeated use of alcohol results in the development of tolerance, and larger doses must then be taken in order to procure characteristic effects.... The alcohol addict still has an upper limit of tolerance, which is usually only 3 or 4 times the amount of alcohol that can be taken by the occasional drinker." Goldberg's studies on tolerance, summarized in J.H. Gaddam, *Lectures on the Scientific Basis of Medicine* (1954–55), vol. 4, p. 241, indicate that "A given degree of intoxication would cost the average heavy drinker about 2.5 times as much as it would cost the average abstainer." Jetter's studies, summarized *id.* at p. 247 (and see QJSA, vol. 3, pp. 475 ff.), showed that the toughest 10% of his subjects could stand 5 times as much alcohol as the 10% with the weakest heads. Dr. Rabinowitch, writing in the *Canadian Bar Review* for 1951, vol. 31, p. 1072, states: "I have seen intoxication ... with values as low as 0.05%.... On the other hand, I have also seen persons with alcohol levels of 0.168%, 0.21%, 0.273% and higher who showed no evidence of intoxication." (See also *QJSA,* vol. 2, p. 35 (1941).)
>
> Mirsky, Piker, Rosenbaum, and Lederer, in their study of "Adaptation of the Central Nervous Systems to Varying Concentrations of Alcohol in the Blood," *QJSA,* vol. 2, p. 35 and pp. 43–44 (1941), concluded that the evidence "casts considerable doubt on the validity of the use of the alcohol concentration in the blood as an index of intoxication

It is apparent that, given a blood alcohol (concentration) of 200 mg. percent (0.20% on the Company's scale) or higher, the only deduction that is permissible is that the subject may have been drunk at some time up to the moment the blood sample was drawn, and not necessarily that the subject was drunk at that moment." . . . Goodman and Gilman, p. 106, conclude that generally an alcohol concentration of 0.20% "is associated with mild to moderate intoxication. In some individuals, of course, this level does not indicate drunkenness, and it must be viewed merely as an average. Obviously, the laboratory data must be interpreted in the light of results of clinical examination." Loftus reached the same conclusion after a study of all automobile drivers in Oslo, Norway, examined over a period of 15 years because of police suspicions. See the translation of his report in *QJSA*, vol. 18, pp. 217 ff. (1957). He also recognized that he was dealing with a "loaded sample," i.e., "those who have behaved in such a way as to attract the attention of the police. The percentage of persons diagnosable (as) not sober is likely to be higher in such a sample than in an average group with corresponding blood alcohol levels." (*Id.* at p. 228.) . . .

It should be stressed that the reports upon which the Company relies for its 0.15% test were intended to apply only in the case of automobile drivers. Even those reports, to quote from the National Safety Council, warned us, "The results of a chemical analysis should not be the sole criterion upon which an official judgment is based. The results of a chemical test should be employed to confirm conclusions drawn from clinical and physical diagnoses. It is also emphasized that arbitrary deductions based upon the so-called '0.15% percent line demarcation' be avoided." As the British Medical Association stated in its 1954 report . . . at p. 22: "The responses of different individuals to the same concentration of alcohol in the tissues vary widely. General statements cannot be safely applied in individual cases; neither should a diagnosis rely solely on the results of laboratory tests. An examining practitioner should base his opinion in the first instance solely on his clinical findings, modified subsequently, if necessary, in the light of the results of any laboratory tests."[50]

Falsification

Arbitrators appear to agree generally that some discipline is warranted when an employee is proved to have falsified time or production records or employment applications. However, it must be shown that the act was a deliberate one with intent to defraud rather than a mere oversight or lapse of memory.

The distortion of a work record may manifest itself in a variety of ways, ranging from manipulation of time cards to misrepresentation of production counts.

A union steward's time card was punched earlier than the time he actually came in, but the steward contended he himself had punched the card at the earlier hour. Despite the fact that he may not have been to blame initially, it was held that the company could fire him because he knowingly became a party to the violation by permitting it. In another case, an employer was held to have properly fired an employee for punching the card of a fellow worker along with his own when no explanation was provided for the fact that both cards had been punched at the same time and the other man had not punched his own.[51]

The misrepresentation may involve work time during the day. At the General Electric Company, a union shop committee chairman persisted in marking on his production work slip time that he had actually spent on union business and should have indicated on a separate slip. The contract contained specific provisions relating to time that union officials spent during working hours on union business and limiting the amount that would be paid for. The union officer had been warned about this practice on several occasions by a number of supervisors and officials of the company before he was disciplined with a one-week layoff. Arbitrator Daniel Kornblum upheld the suspension.[52]

Falsifying a production record does more than increase a company's direct overhead dishonestly. Among other things, it distorts inventory records and production costs, interferes with scheduling and the equitable allocation of work assignments, impedes the development of fair performance credits and earning opportunities, and plays havoc with the sound administration of a wage incentive plan if one exists.

One form of production falsification is "banking," or undercounting the work actually performed during a given time. This was the accusation of the Harnischfeger Corporation against an employee it discharged for failing to report production amounting to more than 24 standard hours' credit. The worker had been warned against the practice just one week earlier under a plant rule against "falsification of records, reports or applications for employment." Taking the man's prior disciplinary record of suspensions and warnings for other offenses into account, Arbitrator Harold M. Gilden upheld the company's action.

At Singer Company, an employee was discharged for the opposite offense of overreporting his production count. He admitted claiming 1,600 pieces when in fact an audit found the count to be 1,382. Although the grievant was aware of his overage throughout the entire workday, he never attempted to correct his error until he saw the checker moving parts to the scale to make an audit. The arbitrator, Sidney L. Cahn, found this timing significant, coupled with the employee's knowledge of the overage, which on too many occasions during the day he "conveniently forgot to change." The company's action was sustained.[53]

Falsifying a job application may be considered a somewhat different matter from distorting production or work records. The present consensus among arbitrators is that it should not be considered justification for peremptory discharge after some reasonable time; a lengthy period of satisfactory employment following the falsification is usually viewed as a bar to a subsequent discharge for that single error.[54] This is particularly true where the facts that are falsified are not of a nature to endanger present or future work relationships.

Misrepresentation on job applications seems to be a rather common practice; in fact, most employers expect applicants to highlight their strengths and good points and soft-pedal their shortcomings. However, if it involves material facts that would have led the company to find the worker unsuitable for employment, it may constitute a serious enough consideration for discharge to be justified. For example, a company could fire an employee who had omitted half his former jobs from his application and had not stated he had been sued three times if the form specifically asked for this information and warned that any falsification or omission would be cause for dismissal. One expert has stated the issue in these words:

> Arbitrators have sought past reported cases to distinguish what matters and what does not matter in falsified or omitted statements on employment applications. Minor details and slips of memory do not matter; a few days worked here or there not mentioned, the name of an elementary school wrongly given, a date far back in the past not rightly remembered (all) come under this heading. The things that matter are those that might well have led to a different decision about the hiring of an employee had the Employer known the full facts at the time....[55]

At the Diamond Power Specialty Corporation, as a case in point, an employee was discharged for having failed to give truthful answers to questions on the job application regarding former work injuries and compensation claims. It was quite clear that the grievant had not answered the questions properly or correctly. He had said that he had never applied for workmen's compensation whereas he had in fact filed eight claims with the Industrial Commission of Ohio over a three-year period. He had answered that he had no type of back injury whereas one of the claims submitted to the commission was for a strained back. In the arbiter's opinion, it was not pertinent whether the falsification was willful; since the information withheld was relevant and material, willfulness was not an element. The arbiter supported the company's action.[56]

A case involving Associated Transport, Inc., was decided the opposite way. The International Association of Machinists protested when management discharged two employees for failing to indicate any permanent physical disabilities. Arbitrator Ralph N. Campbell overturned the action on the grounds that the employees hid nothing from the company doctor, who pronounced both physically qualified, and they acted in the belief that they in fact had no permanent physical disability.[57]

Fights and Altercations

Almost all company rules include a ban on fighting. Fights, heated arguments, and other such disturbances clearly are not conducive to plant harmony and efficiency. But unfortunately, employees do get into fights with each other and their supervisors. Some personal friction appears to be inevitable, rising out of the normal tensions of the industrial work environment. The principles espoused by labor arbitrators on this issue have established a general code of behavior that takes these considerations into account.

It is inherent in the work relationship that personnel must conform to certain well-known, commonly accepted standards of reasonable conduct while on the job. Published rules and regulations are not necessary to inform an employee that misconduct such as fighting and foul language may subject him to discipline or discharge. An industrial plant is a place for the production of goods and the performance of work. While it is not a tearoom, neither is it a place for barroom conduct. Childish, uncontrolled, or irresponsible outbursts accompanied by physical or verbal assault cannot be tolerated. Such behavior is not excusable because the offender is in an agitated emotional state. When an employee lacks the emotional stability and rational judgment to restrain himself from outbursts, he also lacks the minimum qualifications to be retained as a member of the work force.

One or more of the following questions will be found in most arbitral opinions on disputes over discipline for altercations: Was there one aggressor or two in the altercation? What is the employee's past work record? Was the offender's behavior provoked? If a supervisor is involved, did he provoke the employee's behavior, and did he also engage in aggressive conduct himself? If insulting and offensive words were exchanged, did they exceed the norm of shop vernacular for that institution?

The answers to such questions obviously depend on a thorough investigation of the incident by the employer. The question of whether the company has fully investigated the facts before taking disciplinary actions against fighters frequently influences an arbitrator's ruling on a particular penalty.

Where fighting has occurred, arbitrators have reduced discharges to lesser penalties when it was proven that the violence was provoked. In one case, the arbiter said that it was not discriminatory for the employer to discharge the worker who initiated the assault without discharging the one who finally resorted to violence also. Verbal abuse, however, is rarely considered justifiable provocation for a physical response. For example, the laws of Ohio on assault and battery are very clear about this type of incident. It is the generally recognized rule that mere words, however gross, abusive and insulting or however vulgar, vile, or profane, do not justify a physical attack, and are not a defense either to a civil action for damages or to a criminal prosecution growing out of an assault and battery thus provoked.

Most arbitrators will accord with the company position that nothing justifies a physical assault on any employee by anyone, even on the worst and most arbitrary type of supervisor. As put in one opinion, "A plant in the mainstream of production is not unlike a ship afloat. The common necessity for discipline among members of any crew upon which depends so heavily the safety and well-being of all cannot condone mutiny even against a Captain Bligh of *Bounty* notoriety."

The comparison is odious, of course. In no sense are the vast majority of supervisors eligible for categorization in the Captain Bligh mold. The extreme comparison, however, does bring home the point that there are few circumstances that arbiters will consider to justify attacks on supervisors. More often than not, some penalty is upheld, though it may consist of a disciplinary measure short of discharge.

On the other hand, it is also a cardinal rule that supervisors who are attacked should do no more than is sufficient to defend themselves. They should not retaliate or fight back to the point of becoming the aggressor. They should use only the amount of force necessary to fend off the attacker, and at no time should they assume the offensive.

The ruling in the next case was predictable. The grievant was a hot-tempered employee of 14 months' service who was hypersensitive to supervisory direction. He defiantly refused to comply with a normal and reasonable work order to release cases of the company product that were stuck in the conveyor, though this was his responsibility. On being rebuked by his foreman, the grievant flew into a violent rage, knocked the supervisor to the ground, and continued to beat him until forcibly pulled away from him by others. Still not subdued, the attacker shouted, "I'll kill him, I'll kill him." He then seized a heavy wooden case with reinforced metal corners intending to bash the dazed supervisor with it, but he was again restrained by his coworkers. The supervisor, a man of 60, was moved to a hospital for treatment of face and chest injuries. He was confined to bed for five days and to his home for another five days. At the arbitration hearing, the grievant relied exclusively on a decision rendered by the New York State Unemployment Insurance Referee

Section that a worker was properly entitled to unemployment benefits because he was not guilty of misconduct in connection with his work. Needless to say, the discharge was upheld by Arbitrator Burton B. Turkus.[58]

Objectionable Language

What is abusive and offensive language? Under what circumstances will it be cause for discipline, and when will it be overlooked?

In certain types of establishments, bad language is not objectionable in itself. As a matter of fact, it may be objectionable in one portion of the business and not in another. For example, profanity may be rife among waiters in the kitchen, but they speak in a much more restrained manner in the presence of restaurant guests. Along the waterfront, in coal mines, and in garages, the choice of vocabulary is usually less than Chesterfieldian. In other words, the surroundings have a material bearing on the latitude allowed to employees in oral expression.

The tone of voice and the way the language is used can also make a great deal of difference. At the American Ship Building Company, an employee told his foreman, "You're a goddamn liar and always was and will be one." The man's general attitude was belligerent, and he made the statement in the presence of a number of other employees. It even appeared that he had gone out of his way to face the foreman at a place where he had no occasion to be for any purpose. Evidence that the use of profanity between employees and supervisors was not uncommon did not preclude an arbitral finding that the employee's conduct amounted to insubordination.[59]

Arbitrators have often taken note of the degree of influence radiating upon other employees from a man's misconduct in assessing the proper penalty. At Chrysler Corporation, for example, an employee was discharged for using abusive language in threatening a foreman. The discharge was reduced to a disciplinary layoff. The fact that no other employees were present to hear the threat made it unlikely that proper respect for foremen would be endangered by the worker's behavior. A one-week suspension was held not justifiable at the Arkansas Louisiana Chemical Corporation when an employee called a plant superintendent an obscene name, since no other employee heard the exchange and the employee did not boast of it to his coworkers.[60]

Gambling

Most industrial establishments have rules prohibiting gambling on company premises. The reasons are obvious. Time spent in this activity is time lost from production. An employee who suffers gambling losses may take out his frustration and anger on the person he holds responsible. Morale and efficiency are always threatened. The family of the worker who experiences a substantial loss often turns to the employer for comfort and remedy. The employer is always the man in the middle under these circumstances.

Despite the existence of rules or regulations prohibiting it, gambling is prevalent in many places of work. It takes numerous forms. It may be the relatively innocuous baseball pool, check pool, or lunch-hour poker game, or it may be as serious as an organized numbers racket.

There are three basic principles arbitrators tend to observe in evaluating cases of discipline for gambling. First, the evidence connecting the employee with the gambling must be substantial and convincing. Second, discharge is normally viewed as too severe a penalty for the first offense, though not if the employee has been warned previously about gambling. Third, and as an exception to the second principle, discharge is often considered appropriate where the employee has been connected with an organized gambling racket or has engaged in gambling during working hours.

At the Bethlehem Steel Company, management discharged an employee who was apprehended by plant protection officers with $400 in small bills and change and a sheet of lottery numbers. There was no question that the grievant was engaged in unlawful gambling. The fact that his activities were conducted on his own time was immaterial since they were carried out on the employer's premises. The arbiter sustained the company's action.[61]

Another employer was held to be justified in having discharged its newspaper circulation manager for organizing and participating in games run by professional gamblers. The employee knew that his gambling activities were illegal, and the company had warned him to discontinue them. His job was to supervise the work of some 30 carrier boys aged 11 to 15. The company argued that it considered a man in such a position to have a duty to the boys and their parents to maintain a moral atmosphere in the working area. Although there was no evidence that he ever corrupted the boys, it was perfectly obvious to the arbitrator that his conduct drew suspicion on him. After warning him without avail to cease his activities, the company was perfectly justified in concluding that he was not a fit and proper person to supervise boys in their formative years and that he should be discharged for the good of the operation as a whole.[62]

At the Wm. H. Haskell Mfg. Co., management had permitted a turkey raffle at Thanksgiving time for the benefit of the union's social fund and had also agreed that employees could have a World Series pool each year. On the other hand, it had a plant rule providing for immediate discharge of "any employee drinking or gambling on the Company property." Therefore, when the company discovered that a union officer was operating baseball and numbers pools at work, it discharged him. The arbiter supported this action, finding the following factors persuasive: (1) there was no evidence that the discharge was discriminatory; (2) the union officer knew he was taking a calculated risk despite his assertion that his activity was aimed at promoting sociability in the plant; and (3) the one-shot Thanksgiving turkey raffle and annual World Series pools were not comparable to the union officer's gambling schemes, which involved considerable time, daily wagers of substantial sums of money, and outside meetings with promoters of pools and thus had a generally adverse effect on plant production.[63]

Horseplay and Jokes

"Horseplay," as the term is used here, does not mean malicious conduct, but rather playful activities during working hours that, like practical jokes, interfere with plant efficiency, morale, safety, or productivity. Either kind of boisterousness may be the result of chronic euphoria, or it may merely be a momentary (if rough) expression of high spirits. The problem is that too often it causes serious industrial accidents.

In judging disputes over discipline for high jinks, arbitrators are inclined to take into account whether the employee's offense was his first of its kind and what the consequences of the horseplay were. They are as concerned as management with imposing a penalty that has a salutary effect on employees who tend to be frolicsome.

For example, a company disciplined an employee who moved her supervisor's chair as the woman was about to sit down, causing her an injured back that needed a series of medical treatments. The company charged that the act was deliberate, whereas the union asserted that it was not deliberate or intended to cause harm. The arbiter agreed that discipline was warranted but did not accord with the penalty of discharge, which he felt was excessive. The employee's moving of the chair did show lack of judgment, but it was not proved to have been a malicious act. Therefore, he held that a 10-week suspension without pay would impress on the grievant that employees have an obligation to "conduct themselves as mature individuals rather than as lighthearted juveniles."[64]

In a case involving Decar Plastics Corporation, the arbitrator ruled that the company was justified in discharging an employee who became aggrieved at being hit by a piece of hard rubber thrown by other employees and retaliated by placing lit cigarettes in their back pockets, though they operated machines with moving blades and entered spray booths where combustible materials were present. The grievant's conduct involved a high risk of serious injury to others and could not be considered mere horseplay. There were no mitigating circumstances. Despite union arguments, the discharge was not considered discriminatory on the basis of the company's failure to discipline other workers who engaged in horseplay without its specific knowledge.[65]

The next case concerned an employee's behavior, so assaultive, that 14 female co-workers petitioned management to take some corrective action, and the man was discharged for indecent and untoward conduct the next day. In the ensuing grievance hearing, women employees testified to a number of incidents. One said that the grievant had followed her "to the back of the warehouse," where he had "attempted to sexually assault" her and hurt her back in the process, and that he had released her only when two other male employees were attracted to the scene after she cried out that her back was being hurt. Two other women referred also to sexual advances. The grievant denied the first allegation and dismissed the other two incidents as mere horseplay. However, the testimony of another woman at the hearing hardly supported this cavalier attitude: "About three months ago the Grievant came into the ladies' room. He tried to kiss me and tried to lay me on the couch. I told him to leave me alone but he didn't let me go, and then I yelled for the Warehouse Manager and then he let me go and then he just sat there and didn't say anything and then he left. B_____ was there; so was D_____ and E_____." Another charge was that the grievant had recently called a female employee a "blond whore," a remark overheard by three male workers. Other women registered complaints that the grievant had tried to be "unduly friendly" or had made a suggestive and indecent gesture. The man insisted that all the occurrences were just bits of ordinary camaraderie.

It is interesting that despite the evil motivations attributed to the offender, none of the complainants wanted him to be discharged outright. One woman testified that if he remained in his job at the plant, her husband would not allow her to continue to work there. Another said that she was certain her husband was so outraged he would come to the plant and do serious violence to the grievant.

The arbiter nonetheless sustained the grievant's discharge as for good and sufficient cause, stating:

> The Arbitrator has recounted the salient items of testimony and proof in this record at some length because of the seriousness of the charges against the Grievant. Manifestly, an indictment of this nature should not be lightly treated; rather the Employer should be held to something like the measure of proof as obtained in a criminal trial. In this view the Arbitrator is convinced beyond a reasonable doubt that the Grievant was guilty as charged. He is persuaded that the female employees who had direct encounters with the Grievant were genuinely concerned about his misconduct, erotic and otherwise. While he is thoroughly mindful of the fact that a plant such as this is certainly not a finishing school, at the same time it is most unusual for such a sizable group of coworkers in the unit to entreat Management to do something to stop the disturbing conduct of a fellow worker and comember of the Union.[66]

Insubordination

It is presumably a well-established principle that employees are to "obey first and grieve later." Like all general principles, however, this rule has its exceptions.

In the hundreds of cases researched, no penalty whatsoever was permitted by arbitrators in 25 percent of the cases they evaluated. This means that some form of management punishment already imposed, from discharge to some lesser penalty, was disallowed and overturned. In another 40 percent of the cases researched, the arbitrator reduced the penalty to some lesser punishment in light of extenuating circumstances that had not been given sufficient consideration by the employer. In only 25 percent of the cases where discharge had been imposed by the company was this penalty upheld. In 10 percent of the cases a penalty less severe than discharge, as assessed by management, was upheld intact by the outside third party.

These figures demonstrate a very poor batting average by the management team in its arbitral efforts to have its previously taken position of demanding unquestioning obedience upheld. A careful reading of the cases where the company's decision was overruled reflects another factor. In many instances the agents of management were reacting emotionally and sometimes impulsively to employee challenges — questioning, criticism, interference, and the like — of company power and authority.

Insubordination seems to be the form of personal misconduct most often appearing in arbitration hearings. The majority of the cases researched apparently fall into two general categories.

One is the refusal or willful failure to obey orders as issued by representatives of management. The second category comprises cases where employees challenge, criticize, obstruct, abuse, or interfere with management's supervision in various ways. The second category generates the greatest number of lost or compromised arbitral decisions for management. Presuming that an order does not jeopardize the health, safety, or welfare of the employee, or require him to accede to an illegal or immoral demand, that it is reasonably within his capability, and that it does not cause him to lose some other contractual right or benefit, the majority of arbitrators will uphold the doctrine of "Obey first and grieve later." In any case, that appeared to be the supported premise when management's action was upheld by the arbitrator in the cases constituting the first category.

Loafing

Loafing is dealt with here by itself as an issue separate from its companion issue of sleeping because it is often subjected to lesser penalties by arbitrators. Loafing may take many different forms. An employee may spend a lot of time talking with other employees; he may loiter in the rest room, in the vending machine area, or around the water cooler; he may wander from his machine or department into other sections where he does not belong. Whatever the kind of loafing, the result is that the worker is disengaged from his proper productive activity.

It is important in cases of this kind for management to establish that the employee is truly lingering and that his idleness is not legitimate or beyond his control. For example, a supervisor observed a group of employees clustered together and talking 55 minutes before the end of their shift. Disciplinary notices were issued to all these workers. Yet by his own admission, the foreman had actually watched them for no more than 50 seconds. He did not know how long they had been gathered together talking, nor did he inquire. He did not know whether they were discussing a production problem or the previous day's baseball game, nor did he ask them. He surmised that they might have stayed conversing aimlessly until the end of the shift, 55 minutes later. He assumed they were taking advantage of the absence of the foreman to quit work. In short, because he did not investigate the matter, his own testimony disabled the case that he postulated. The employees' grievance was sustained.[67]

Although such cases are in the minority, discharges for a first offense of loafing have been upheld. An arbiter will sustain this penalty when he feels or actually is compelled by the language of the collective bargaining agreement to do so.

An example of this occurred in a dispute arising at the Bethlehem Steel Company. A worker was discharged for loafing on the job after the supervisor, who had searched for him for some time, found him sitting in a restricted area smoking a cigarette. The employee claimed he had been sent to the area by the supervisor, but this man denied the allegation. The arbiter sustained the discharge, commenting:

> The most damaging evidence against the Grievant is his admission that he was caught loafing. Irrespective of how much work he might have performed that evening by comparison with other members of the gang, the fact still remains that he deliberately abandoned his work in order to loaf. He has given as a reason for going to the forepeak area his instruction to obtain a piece of string. Again, the facts show that his Leaderman did not tell him to get any string in the forepeak area, which was an off-limit location. It is obvious X_____ went to this area to escape for a few minutes his work assignment. Finally, there is the matter of severity of penalty. In this case, there can be no question that under the circumstances, the Company had a right to effect the discharge of X_____. Management could have found it desirable to be lenient and grant clemency to X_____ in the interest of generosity toward an unfortunate employee who made a mistake. This was not the case. The Arbitrator has no authority within the nature of the grievance statement to propose now that Management grant clemency to this individual.[68]

The opposite finding was brought by Arbitrator Peter Di Leone in a dispute between the Indiana Desk Company, Inc., and the United Furniture Workers of America. The company discharged some employees who worked on the fourth floor of the plant but had been found shortly before noon waiting on the stairs near the first-floor time clock to punch out for lunch. Management had condoned this practice for many years. When it established a new rule prohibiting the practice, it communicated the change on a hit-or-miss basis. In the arbiter's view, moreover, the nature of the conduct involved suggested that a graduated system of punishment for violation of the rule was appropriate. He therefore reduced the discharges to one-week suspensions.[69]

This case brings home once again the points that rules must be reasonable, uniformly applied, and communicated properly to the employees they affect and that any punishment imposed for violations must fit the crime.

Arbitrator Samuel S. Kates ruled that the Martin Company was justified in discharging one engineer but not the other when both had left a boiler unattended to engage in conversation unrelated to their work. While they were talking in the office adjoining the boiler room, the coupling in the feed pump broke, overheating the boiler. The arbiter held that the discharge penalty was too severe in the case of one of the men, who had had only two months on the job and who had behaved properly on discovering the situation by shutting off the burner and calling for his more experienced companion. Kates upheld the discharge of the other employee because this man had greater knowledge of the risk involved in leaving the boiler room unattended. In addition, he had lost his head on being summoned by the junior employee and pushed a button activating another pump, thereby sending water into the overheated boiler and causing $23,000 worth of damage.[70]

Overtime Work Refused

Under the provisions of labor agreements, it is well established that a company has the right to compel employees to work overtime in the absence of some contractual restriction. It can compromise this general right if its insistence on the overtime is capricious or discriminatory, if its order to the employees has not been clearly and directly communicated or if it has failed to take corrective steps in the face of previous refusals to work overtime.

Two of these points are illustrated by a dispute at Hussman, San Francisco (a Ray Winther Co. subsidiary), which imposed two-day disciplinary suspensions on 10 employees who refused to work emergency overtime. Arbiter James J. Willingham discovered that employees had consistently regarded unposted overtime as voluntary and had not been disciplined for previous refusals. Nor were they warned that they would be disciplined if they refused to work. Moreover, the evidence on whether the grievants were given a direct order to work overtime was conflicting and did not establish that they were. The arbiter therefore lifted the suspensions.[71]

Arbiter William Stix considered it an implicit obligation in a contract's grievance procedure for employees to accept the company's directives, even if disputed, and to grieve later. Therefore, a worker who rejected an overtime assignment was manifesting a do-it-yourself approach to a shop controversy that, like a collective work stoppage, constituted a direct challenge to the employer's authority. Accordingly, the arbitrator upheld the company's two-day disciplinary layoff of employees who refused overtime work even though they believed that the assignment violated the contract.

Several arbiters have overruled discipline imposed on employees who declined to work on Christmas and New Year's Eve. As one opinion phrased it, these are "peculiar and sacred" holidays in our culture;

therefore, the refusal to work on these overtime days is not a punishable offense since workers would suffer an irretrievable loss not recoverable under the concept of "work now, grieve later."[72]

Still other umpires have ruled that discipline was inappropriate where one or more of the following factors have been involved: (1) the amount of overtime required is excessively large; (2) the overtime work is not of the emergency type, and other workers are conveniently available; (3) no effort is made to obtain other employees more willing after those first assigned the work have declined; and (4) the overtime is announced so late that affected employees have insufficient time to adjust their personal schedules for transportation and other needs.[73]

Physical or Mental Disability

Arbitrators generally recognize management's right to discharge an employee who is physically unable to do the job, particularly if no other suitable positions are available. The case is often decided on the basis of medical testimony. The overwhelming majority of companies call on doctors they employ or select to make medical judgments of an employee's condition and his ablity to perform his work. Arbiters generally uphold management's prerogative to rely on the opinion of its doctors, but they do consider that the employee has a right to introduce the conflicting opinion of his own medical adviser before the company's action becomes final.

Most arbitrators are not medically trained, so that it is often extremely difficult for them to resolve differences between the conclusions of the company's and the employee's doctors. Management is usually well advised to attempt to reconcile such differences in advance of the arbitration proceedings. It might have the company doctor discuss the matter with the employee's doctor. If this brings no reconciliation of opinion, the two physicians might jointly select a colleague to answer the questions between them and agree that the parties would be bound by his conclusions.

The dilemma of the arbitrator who must resolve differences of opinion between two competent medical authorities was aptly expressed by Israel Ben Scheiber:

> Just as in the words of the inimitable Gilbert and Sullivan, a policeman's lot is not a happy one, so too, a layman who is called on to decide sharply conflicting testimony by members of the medical profession is placed in a most unhappy situation, especially where the potentials of his decision may be a serious impact on the parties who depend on his good judgment.[74]

A review of a large number of awards involving discharge because of physical disability shows that the most material issue to arbitrators is whether the company's action has been arbitrary, capricious, or unreasonable.

This question arose in a grievance against Atlas Chemical Industries, Inc., by the International Chemical Workers Union. Arbitrator LeRoy Autrey concluded that the company had not acted arbitrarily or unreasonably in discharging an employee suffering from pulmonary difficulties. Despite a conflict in specific medical findings, five doctors recommended that he not be allowed to work in a dusty atmosphere, and no contrary medical judgment was advanced. The evidence indicated that he was not qualified for any job with the company other than as a truck driver, which exposed him to considerable lignite dust.[75]

An employee's own doctor's conclusions can lead to his discharge. At the Goss Company, a man submitted a claim for disability benefits under the employer's insurance program, accompanying it by a statement from his own physician that he was permanently disabled. The company thereupon terminated his employment. The union argued that the employer was obliged to seek other medical opinion, and at the arbitration hearing, which came three months after the discharge, it submitted another doctor's statement that the employee was capable of performing full-time work. Arbitrator Albert A. Epstein upheld the termination on the grounds that the procedure followed by the employee was of his own choosing and that the new medical opinion was not relevant to the situation existing at the time of his discharge.[76]

Some chronic conditions, however, are not viewed as a bar to continued employment even though they seem severe. For example, epilepsy in and of itself has generally not been considered cause for discharge. In several disputes that involved the employment of epileptics, arbitrators have held against discharge where there was no compelling evidence of any safety hazard attendant on the affliction.

Cases involving mental illness are difficult to categorize. Most employers hesitate to reemploy a person who has suffered a mental illness. This is particularly so where the fear exists that it may recur. Despite their recognition of this, arbitrators have refused to uphold discharges where there was medical evidence that the employee had recovered at least to the extent that his return to work would not constitute an undue risk.

Immoral conduct may be caused by mental illness. In disputes involving discharge for this reason, arbitrators have directed reinstatement when evidence has been provided that the illness has been cured. However, such awards have been based in part on the fact that the employee's fellow workers had no objection to his reinstatement.

The question of narcotics addiction, which has both physical and mental effects, has aroused increasing concern in the industrial community as in society at large during recent years. One arbitrator, looking to the rapid deterioration caused by drug abuse, held the Chicago Pneumatic Tool Company to be justified in having discharged an employee who pleaded guilty to charges of obtaining narcotics through fraud and deceit and who was found to be addicted to cocaine. The arbiter reasoned that the addict's state, though the result of off-duty conduct, affected the employment relationship in that his degeneration could at any time reach the point where it would seriously endanger the health and safety of fellow employees and company equipment.[77]

Safety

Employers generally recognize their obligation to provide a safe and healthful working place for their employees. The degree to which they fulfill this requirement varies. Regrettably, there are companies that do not give so much attention to this aspect of their business as they do to such matters as production, quality, and schedules. Too many seem to feel that this responsibility can always be deferred to another time, and too often that time comes only when complaints or accidents rise critically or the current disposable income of the business is large.

Many employers, on the other hand, consistently consider the health and safety of their workers among their highest priorities. Again regrettably, not enough credit is given these firms for their commendable commitment. Their reasons are both practical and humane. The factor of practicality relates to such considerations as insurance premium costs, workmen's compensation expenses, and reputation in the manpower marketplace. The humane factor speaks for itself.

Safety, health, and sanitary conditions are naturally always of concern to any labor organization that represents the employer's workers. In addition, there are various municipal, state, and federal laws and regulations that most employers must operate within. It is therefore quite common for a labor agreement to contain some form of pledge from the company that it will give attention to these aspects of working conditions. A few examples of such contract clauses provide a sampling of their variety.

One provision states the employer's intention to conform with any applicable statutes or regulations: "The Management agrees to provide and maintain proper safety and sanitary devices throughout its plants, in accordance with Federal, State and local standards." Another contract reads: "The Employer agrees to comply with all standards of sanitation provided by the New Jersey State laws. The Employer agrees to conduct fire drills in accordance with the requirement of the New Jersey State law."

Frequently found are provisions that explicitly specify the company's responsibilities concerning the health and safety of its employees. These clauses are common even when the employer is not embraced by government regulations, which means that he is voluntarily accepting the obligation. The following are examples:

> The company will make provisions for the safety and health of the employees during the hours of their employment. Protective devices and other equipment necessary to protect the employees from injury, or safeguard their health, will be provided by the Company and all employees will abide by the safety rules and regulations. The Company will have a nurse in attendance in the First Aid Hospital at all times when there are any employees working in the plant.
>
> The Company will make adequate provisions for the safety and health of the employees, and will supply special safety equipment necessary to properly protect employees from injury without cost to the employee where the necessity for such equipment is agreed upon by the Company and the Union.

It goes without saying that neither the inclusion of provisions like these nor the employer's utmost efforts alone will insure a safe and healthful working place. A great part of the responsibility for achieving this end rests with the employee and the union, whose cooperation is expressly solicited in some contracts. Unsafe and unwise acts committed by workers can produce accidents, even disaster, in the safest environment. Unfortunately, it is sometimes necessary for management to exercise its disciplinary authority to bring this point to its workers.

In contrast, employees sometimes refuse to perform work because, they contend, it will jeopardize their own or other workers' safety, health, or welfare. The refusal may actually be well founded: there may be a genuine risk present that can be demonstrated. But at best, the worker who raises such an objection is treading on uncertain ground.

The delicate nature of this question is evidenced in a dispute at the Wilcolator Co., where a walkout occurred over a presumed health hazard. Arbiter James V. Altieri concluded that the employees' belief, though sincere, was not sufficient justification for the walkout, for they had not established that the hazard did in fact exist.[78]

Each case brought to arbitration that concerns an employee's accident record is judged on its individual merits, as are disputes based on all other issues. But it is possible to encapsulate general concepts that influence arbitral conclusions.

The majority of arbitrators look askance at a management's contention that a discharge has been imposed because an employee is "accident prone." The comments of Arbiter Alexander H. Frey summarize the attitude in the profession toward such a claim:

> [I]ndustrial discipline, especially the supreme penalty of discharge, should not be based upon the conclusion that a given employee is "accident prone." Without having been careless or negligent, a driver may be involved in a series of accidents for which he is blameless; if so, there is no basis for punishment. A driver may drive illegally or recklessly and luckily escape accidents for a period of time; such a driver merits discipline....[79]

When an employee is discharged because of his accident record, the requirement of just cause makes it incumbent upon the company to prove that he was culpably careless or negligent, not merely an involved party. Another factor is the seriousness of the accident that results in discharge. If worse incidents have been excused or given lesser disciplinary penalties, discharge will generally be considered too severe for a subsequent accident of smaller consequence.

In the dispute decided by Frey, both these factors are revealed. A truck driver for the Interstate Bakeries Corporation was discharged after his fourth accident. Two previous ones had not been his fault; a serious one that was attributable to his negligence had brought him a suspension. The fourth accident, nearly nine months later, was relatively minor and did not clearly involve negligence on his part. Given these particulars, the arbitrator viewed the discharge as "manifestly unfair" and reinstated the driver without loss of seniority and with back pay to the date of his discharge minus four weeks.

Just as involvement in an accident would not establish an employee's responsibility for it and thus justify his discharge, nor would cancellation of the company's insurance coverage or a substantial increase in its premiums. This was the issue in a dispute over the discharge of a truck driver three weeks after he had been involved in an accident. During the three-week period, he had continued to work and carry out driving assignments. The company discharged him the same day it received a letter from its insurance carrier asserting that the employee had been negligent and threatened the cancellation of its coverage if he was not fired. In the arbitration hearing, management offered no evidence that the grievant had been at fault in any way — neither it nor the insurance company had made any investigation of the accident — but claimed it had an established policy of dismissing any driver who had an accident, regardless of fault. The arbitrator commented, "We need not pass on the propriety of such a rule, when the evidence made clear that discharges were not triggered by accidents but by letters from the insurance company. Indeed, this is evident from the fact that the grievant was allowed to continue driving for nearly three weeks after the accident, but was discharged immediately when the letter arrived."[80]

A case involving the McLouth Steel Corp. contained two elements that constituted problems to the arbitrator in reaching his conclusions: The employee's accident record and the fact that the company had demoted the offender rather than disciplining or discharging him. The employee, a crane operator, had three safety incidents in the space of 16 months. The first was apparently of a kind that is not uncommon. The second was more serious in that the grievant ignored or was unaware of the danger to which he subjected a fellow employee. The third was the most serious because it highlighted his apparent inability to take into account factors that are fundamental in operating a crane safely. A welder was repairing a furnace roof in the area where the crane was working, and though he was out of sight under the roof, a red light signaled his presence. Despite this, the grievant attempted to set down the crane bucket, which was about 10 feet in diameter and 13 feet high. It struck the roof, dislodging some of the roof bricks. The worker's welding shield was pinned by the bricks and broken, but he slipped out of the hood and fell to the floor, escaping injury. This incident brought about the crane operator's demotion to general labor.

After considering these circumstances and with the safety of all the workers in mind, the arbitrator did not believe he should reverse the action of the company officials directly responsible for and intimately acquainted with the day-to-day operations of the plant. After all, the best evidence of a safe operator is the absence of accidents.[81]

The next case is interesting for the reason that an employee's failure to report accidents was as instrumental in his discharge as were the accidents themselves. The employer, Thiokol Chemical Corporation, operated a government plant producing a critical product, which made strict adherence to rules a necessity. The grievant was discharged following the last of three incidents, none of which endangered lives directly or cost great sums of money but none of which he reported to the supervisor, as well-known company regulations required. He had been suspended for the same failure on two prior occasions. With the third offense — neglecting to report that he had installed the wrong structural steel beam in a plant building — he was discharged.

Arbitrator Marion Beatty remarked, "It is the employee's refusal to report such incidents that I believe justifies the Company's deciding this employee is not a safe and proper person to have on its premises." The grievance was denied.[82]

A large number of arbitration cases over the issue of safety involve company truck drivers. The dangers of operating a vehicle are obvious from the national statistics on injuries, deaths, and property losses from road and highway accidents. In fact, trucking concerns, recognizing this occupational hazard, commonly adopt contractual provisions that express particular concern about driving safety.

Arbitrators show this same concern by their reluctance to disturb disciplinary discharges for accidents where it means returning an employee to the highway who may be dangerous or where the company's legal and financial welfare is at stake. Within this framework, arbiters have generally upheld discharges of drivers who have had numerous accidents and/or a poor past record, as in the following cases:

1. Four accidents in 10 months and a driving record significantly worse than other drivers' (Standard Oil Company of California).[83]

2. Six accidents in three years (Ward Baking Company).[84]

3. Five accidents within one year (Chevy Chase Dairy).[85]

4. An extremely bad past record and one serious accident (Hudson County Bus Owners Assoc.).[86]

5. A serious pattern of speeding that caused a third accident (Schreiver Company Trucking).[87]

6. Seven accidents in five years with a persistently deteriorating accident record (Kroger Company).[88]

On the other hand, the penalty of discharge has been set aside and reinstatement ordered (usually without back pay) under the following circumstances:

1. Negligence not conclusively shown for a second accident in six months, which the arbiter saw as the result of a "moment of inadvertence" and not "willful misconduct or gross negligence" (Safe Bus Company, Inc.), and

2. No danger to the public (Safe Bus Company, Inc.).[89]

3. Ordinary negligence, as distinguished from gross negligence or willful or wanton conduct (American Synthetic Rubber Corp.).[90]

Sleeping

Proving an employee was sleeping is a most difficult task. The excuses offered are a tribute to human inventiveness. They range from praying to meditating (with closed eyes) on the sterling attributes of the supervisor who has caught the sleeper in the act.

Because they recognize the complications of proving a worker was sleeping, many managers choose instead to call the offense "neglect of duty," "inattention to appointed tasks with resulting hazards to safety," or some other locution appropriate to the circumstances. If there is evidence that the worker was in such a relaxed or supine physical state that he was not fulfilling his responsibilities, an arbitrator will usually not require that actual sleeping be proved.

Whatever the charge, it is always beneficial to the company's case if the employee's behavior has been witnessed by more than one person. It may be able to prove he was indeed asleep if witnesses can testify that they woke him or stood beside him until he awoke. They may reasonably conclude that he is sleeping, said Arbitrator Carl A. Warns in a Lockheed Aircraft Corp. case, when he is in repose with his eyes closed and is unresponsive during several minutes of close observation.[91]

An employee's disciplinary record and length of service are frequently taken into consideration in grievance hearings on this issue. Arbitrators seem inclined to reduce discharges to suspensions without pay when the offending employee has a combination of a clear work history and several years of good and faithful service. This is particularly true when it is the worker's first offense.

The nature of the employee's job also has a bearing on the arbitral conclusions. For example, sleeping while on duty is a more serious matter for a plant guard than a materials clerk. Therefore, arbiters would be more likely to uphold a discharge for the guard's first offense than the clerk's, and would do so even if the guard had an exceptionally good personal record.

Where an established rule or practice regarding sleeping has been consistently and uniformly applied to erring workers and where the penalty has been discharge, arbiters will generally uphold that action as proper. They will do so as well even if no specific rule is in force if the offense involves some danger to the safety of employees or a hazard to equipment.

Theft

There is little question that stealing constitutes an offense warranting discharge and is consequently one of the gravest acts of which an employee may be accused or found guilty. In fact, it is so serious that rarely does any specific warning precede a discharge decision.

Challenging the fairness or propriety of a rule against stealing is an exercise in futility for a union. Arbitral reaction to such an attempt is best summed up in a decision brought down by Arbitrator Paul Lehoczky:

> Rules that represent simple translations of the laws (common or statute) which set up the public code of conduct (physical violence, destruction,

immoral acts, etc., and including theft) cannot be ruled as "unfair" as compared to rules dealing with smoking, garnishment of wages and the like, peculiar to the operation of the enterprise in question.[92]

Unlike misconduct that relates uniquely to the working place, such as absenteeism, loafing, and insubordination, stealing is also reprehensible in the whole of society. The person who takes a job brings with him the prior knowledge that stealing is a crime against society and that it is equally a crime against his employer.

Because of the gravity of this offense and its threat to the name and reputation of one found guilty of it, arbitrators impose a heavy burden of proof on the accusing party. It is probably for this reason also that they overturn a large majority of discharges for theft. Practitioners disagree on the quantum of proof that is required of an employer, but most would likely concur that a higher degree of proof than the "preponderance of the evidence," which is the approach used most frequently in arbitration proceedings, is usually required when the alleged misconduct is of a kind recognized and punished by the criminal law.

The reluctance of arbiters to uphold discharge actions for stealing unless the evidence is compelling is understandable. The person found guilty not only loses his job with his present employer but may very well be stigmatized in the eyes of the entire industrial community within his locale, and the public knowledge of his prosecution may bring social injury to his family. Arbiters cannot be faulted for proceeding with concern and caution.

Reviewing the rulings in a few cases will highlight how arbitrators treat the question of sufficient proof.

In a dispute at the Great Atlantic & Pacific Tea Co., Inc., Arbiter Marlin Volz held that the company did not have just cause for discharging an employee who was seen emerging from a meat cooler with a package of dried beef in his hand and who failed to offer an immediate explanation. The worker made no effort to conceal the package, and the story he subsequently provided for why he had the package remained consistent when he retold it. His record was good and clean and contained no prior charge of pilferage. The arbiter ruled that the evidence did not establish guilt of theft clearly and convincingly. However, he did believe that the worker was guilty of unauthorized possession of company property, for which a two-week suspension without pay would be an appropriate penalty.[93]

Arbitrator Burton B. Turkus supported the discharge of an employee by United Parcel Service, Inc., on the basis of independent, clear, and convincing evidence that the man had participated in the theft of $200,000 in money orders. His refusal to testify was a proper exercise of his constitutional protection against self-incrimination, particularly since criminal proceedings against him were then pending, and no implication of guilt or innocence was attached to his silence. But that privilege did not guarantee him reinstatement in his job when independent evidence of his dishonesty established his guilt.[94]

4. Off-Duty Reasons for Discipline

The majority of offenses that would bring down discipline were they to occur on the job are not subject to company action if they happen off the job, off company premises, and during nonworking time. Generally, the employer is not entitled to take issue with a worker's off-duty behavior, for this would constitute invasion of his privacy and curtailment of his freedom of action. However, certain kinds of conduct may be construed as so closely related to job activities or relationships that they compel management's attention, and arbiters have upheld employers who have disciplined workers found guilty of them.

Off-duty activities that have been considered to be eligible for company discipline include the following:

1. Behavior that harms the company's reputation or product.

2. Pursuit of a job feud outside the plant with a very real risk of a renewal of the feud back on the job, or assault that clearly arises out of the working relationship between the employees and not out of personal differences.

3. Conduct that makes other employees reluctant or unable to work with the offender.

4. Conduct that evinces a dangerous propensity, a criminal tendency, or serious emotional instability in the employee and that is likely to manifest itself on the job.

5. Off-duty behavior that shows the employee to be a bad industrial risk.

6. Conditions that impair the efficiency or attendance of the worker, such as alcoholism.

Competition with the Employer

While resolving a dispute between Radio Buffalo, Inc., and the National Association of Broadcast Employees and Technicians, Arbitrator Peter Seitz made the following observations:

> The relationship of employer and employee is one of mutual trust and confidence. An employer, in consideration of [the] duties and obliga-

71

tions which he owes to the employee, is entitled to the assurance that the employee will not engage in interests damaging to the enterprise. The good faith that is implicit in and is an inarticulate premise of every contract guarantees that. Such an assurance does not need expression in the contract. In its absence, it is reasonable and proper for an employer to promulgate a rule or regulation prohibiting "conflict of interest" activities. Lacking any general rule, an employer may find other appropriate means of bringing it home to an employee that his outside activities on behalf of a competing employer are detrimental to the enterprise and inconsistent with his duties as an employee.[95]

Thus, even when no written instrument expresses it, a principle underlying the employment relationship is that a worker will not conduct himself in a manner detrimental to the interests of his employer. Most companies assume that each employee will engage only in activities that will promote the welfare of the organization supporting him. After all, his livelihood is derived from that relationship, and it is ill advised to bite the hand that feeds one.

Sometimes, employers promulgate rules that forbid outside activities such as moonlighting, an offense that will be treated separately later in this chapter. Or the rules may state that employees will be subject to discipline if they commit acts of disloyalty or engage in pursuits that compete with the employer's operations. When a company believes a worker is doing something that is a real or potential threat to its interests, it attempts to curtail this by punishing the offender.

The reasonableness of such rules is often in contention and is usually determined on the basis of how broad their scope is. Arbiters tend to look askance at rules that appear to maintain an arbitrary control over employees after work. But where a rule is specifically limited in its application to the performance of similar outside work, it is generally viewed as having been designed explicitly and uniquely to maintain the well-being of the company. This has been the holding where such rules have been challenged by the union.

Several factors usually have a bearing on the outcome of a dispute over an allegation of competitive work. Most of these are common to other types of disciplinary issues, such as whether a rule existed, whether it was generally made known to the employees, and whether it was uniformly and regularly applied. Some questions are peculiar to this issue: Was the action of the offender a real or only a potential threat to the company? Did the company in fact experience some injury?

A number of these factors influenced the arbitrator's decision in a case involving the New York Central Railroad Company (now Penn Central Transportation Company). A yardman it employed also practiced law on the side. For several years, he had acted as attorney for fellow employees in prosecuting claims for personal injury damages against the carrier. He had done this with the company's knowledge, but ultimately it became offended at the practice and discharged him. However, there was no specific rule covering activities like his, and there was no evidence that in its absence any prior warning had been issued to him. Arbitrator Hubert Wyckoff commented:

> There is ancient authority for the proposition that a man cannot serve two masters; and as a lawyer the claimant must have been fully aware of this principle. . . .
> There is no rule in this Labor Agreement, and the Carrier has not issued a specific rule, that will support the charge made here. This is not necessarily fatal, for there are certain types of conduct such as murdering passengers or wrecking trains that could hardly be condoned for the want of a rule.
> The difficulty with this case is that, with the Carrier's knowledge, Claimant has previously engaged in the conduct for which he is now dismissed without any charge ever before having been lodged against him by the Carrier. Whatever may have been the Carrier's reasons for not charging him in the prior cases, in the absence of a specific rule, Claimant was at least entitled to a warning; and there is no evidence that he ever received one.[96]

Thus holding, the arbitrator ordered the reinstatement of the worker but without payment for time lost. This certainly put the employee on notice. He now had been warned. If he practiced law again, it would surely lead to his permanent dismissal.

There is some disagreement over whether the employer must establish that the business was indeed harmed by the worker's outside activities. Arbitrator John E. Gorsuch is one expert who has subscribed to the philosophy that there need be no direct demonstration of actual damage to the principal employer since the very situation itself is injurious to him.[97]

The arbitrator in the following matter was from the same school. A company that fabricated various types of aluminum bodies for trucks discharged an employee for assisting his brother in a small aluminum welding business that also included the building of aluminum truck bodies. At the arbitration hearing, the company stated that it had lost work valued at $9,000 to $12,000 in a three-month period as a result of the competition from this concern. The shop rules contained a rule that engaging in business competitive with the company's products would be considered cause for discharge. The company pointed to the likelihood that association by its employees with competitors would give those firms access to valuable information regarding design and production techniques, including engineering and experimental work developed by it at considerable expense and effort, and that this could enable the competitors to undercut its established prices. It also expressed the fear that knowledge gained at its plant might be used for contacting customers in order to obtain orders, a fear enhanced by the fact that such information was readily available to employees in the grievant's classification.

The arbiter made some highly lucid observations that indicate the prevailing arbitral opinion on this issue:

> It is a well-recognized principle in industrial relations that an employee should not engage in outside employment which suggests a conflict of interest and divided loyalty. It would be manifestly unfair for an employee to work for an Employer during the day and for a competitor evenings, particularly where the work performed for the latter could reasonably involve the use of technical information, skills, and techniques acquired as a result of the employment relationship. To do so would constitute a situation of indirect competition between the employee and his employer, and would be violative of the implied conditions of employment which are inherent in the relationship. . . .
>
> In situations involving conflict of interests, it is not necessarily required that the Employer convincingly establish that a business detriment or financial loss has in fact resulted; it is sufficient if the off-duty relationship is such as would reasonably suggest that the outside employment would lead to a disclosure to the competitor of information and skills acquired by the employee, and this is particularly true when the competing employer is engaged in a similar type of business and in the same general geographical area. The situation would tend to destroy the element of confidence which an employer must have, and would inhibit the disclosure of production information, engineering skills, and procedures. Information acquired through the ingenuity, research, and financial expenditures of an employer should not be siphoned off through the back door by employees whose loyalties are divided between their employer and its competitors.[98]

It was the conclusion of this chairman that the enterprise for which the grievant worked part time was in direct competition with the employer and that this gave rise to a conflict of interest. The discharge was sustained.

This was not a case of mere moonlighting, which is distinguishable. Rules against moonlighting are mainly concerned with the division of an employee's energies between two employers. The situation considered above was an intolerable one for the employer and constituted a breach of an implied condition of employment as well as of a plant rule.

An employee of the Babcock & Wilcox Company was indicted on the charge of contributing to the delinquency of a minor, which is a misdemeanor under Pennsylvania law. He subsequently pleaded guilty and was sentenced to imprisonment for six months. Midway in its term, he was released and placed on parole for the remainder of his sentence. While in jail, he was notified by the company that he was discharged.

His prior record as an employee was good, and the incident occurred off plant premises and outside of working hours. The union grieved and the matter was arbitrated. The pertinent comments of Arbitrator Duff are as follows:

> Even if Grievant's conduct is viewed in its most undesirable light, there is no relationship between the offense and Grievant's status as an employee. Grievant did not tend to corrupt the morals of any employee.... There is no reason why any fellow employee would have any reluctance to continue working with Grievant. The Plant Rule which prohibits "Conduct which violates the common decency or morality of the community" is reasonable and enforceable so long as it is applied to conduct which directly relates to the employer-employee relationship. This Rule cannot authorize the Company to punish off-duty conduct of employees who violate the criminal code of the Commonwealth, unless such infractions are related to the business of the Company. The evidence fails to prove any relationship between this unsavory incident in Grievant's private life and his usefulness as an employee....[99]

It is clear that this was a situation where the employee's improper behavior while functioning in society on his own time did not have any impact on the employer-employee relationship. Duff reinstated him in his former position without back pay.

As a testimony to consistency, the same arbitrator reaffirmed the pertinent concept and upheld a discharge in a case involving Robertshaw Controls Company and the Steelworkers Union. The reprehensible conduct was sexual perversion with youngs boys of the community, and the facts indicated that a discernible relationship did exist between the criminal acts and the status of the grievant as an employee.[100]

A worker had been employed by the New Haven Gas Company for approximately seven years. He was charged with embezzlement in connection with his part-time employment by a laundromat. After pleading guilty, he was given a six-month suspended sentence and placed on probation for two years. As a result of the conviction, he was discharged by the gas company. In support of its action, the company pointed out that it was a public utility and as such was expected by its customers to maintain higher standards among its employees than other enterprises whose position did not directly affect the public interest. It had in its possession 3,500 keys to customers' premises for use by meter readers and servicemen in the event no one was at home. Although the grievant did not have either of these positions, the labor agreement did permit him to exercise his seniority to take one of the jobs if he was qualified to perform it.

The union argued that the crime had nothing to do with the

employee's work for the gas company. He lost no time from work as a result of his arrest and conviction. The utility was acting as if it owned an employee for 24 hours a day.

In the arbitrator's view, the overriding consideration was the public nature of the company's business and the position of trust its personnel must maintain with the public. The public was not aware that the grievant did not have access to customers' homes or keys. Moreover, he could transfer to one of the jobs that would make the keys available to him. In view of these factors and the nature of the employee's crime, the arbiter ruled that the company had proper cause to discharge him.[101]

A dairy was held to be justified in having suspended a route salesman charged with pandering and obscene exhibition even though the arrest occurred while he was on vacation and the contract did not impose off-duty ethical or moral standards on members of the unit. This was the ruling of Arbiter Charles L. Mullin, Jr., who expressed the opinion that insofar as management bears responsibility for meeting competition and maintaining goodwill, it alone is to estimate the possibility of an employee's continuing to perform as a salesman. The fact that the name of the dairy and the man's occupational identity were withheld in newspaper account was not significant. The arrest was publicized in the relatively small town where he lived and where his route was located. Thus he would be inescapably recognized by his name and identified by his customers in his capacity as one of the dairy's salesmen.[102]

It should be treated as a valid proposition that discipline may rightly be imposed when an incident occurring off company property has its roots at the plant and is clearly related or prejudicial to working conditions in the factory. Such is the case with fights or attacks generated by a feud between two or more employees.

An employee of the United States Steel Corporation went to his supervisor's home, complained of a remark the supervisor had made at work, and struck him on the head with a blunt instrument. Although the assault occurred away from the plant and outside of working hours, Arbitrator Sylvester Garrett upheld the discharge of the employee since the dispute stemmed directly from the working relationship in the plant. In so doing, he remarked, "While public authority also is available to deal with those who willfully commit assault and battery, this does not deprive Management of essential authority to maintain discipline and to protect members of supervision from unprovoked reprisals by dissatisfied employees away from work."[103]

The late Harry Shulman, who was permanent arbitrator for Ford Motor Company and the UAW, once pointed out, "The jurisdictional line which limits the company's power of discipline is a functional, not a physical line" and is concerned with the "proximity of the relationship between the conduct and the employment."

There are arbitration precedents for the contention that an employee on his own time and off company property is subject only to the restraints of civil law and not to the authority of the employer. Despite these findings, the established principle is that the employer does have the right to discipline employees for off-duty altercations that are work-related and that are not simply the result of a mutual agreement to settle a matter outside of working hours in the ancient if no longer honorable method of recourse to fists.

Sometimes a dispute that raises the issue of off-duty misconduct will involve an offense committed on company premises. At Inland Container Corporation, an employee who had a longstanding feud with a fellow worker entered the plant intoxicated one day when he was off duty and threatened the other man with a gun. He refused to leave the premises and was finally taken off by the foreman. The employer discharged him. The union argued that the company should have depended on civil authorities to discipline him. Arbitrator D. Emmett Ferguson upheld the company's action on the ground that it could discharge even an off-duty worker if his wrongful acts injured the business. A man's right to personal liberty did not extend to the point of allowing him to invade company property and threaten a fellow employee.[104]

Moonlighting rules are promulgated by a company usually for two reasons. One, as we saw in a previous section, is to keep its employees from working for a competitor and divulging trade secrets. The other is to prevent its employees from engaging in work that has a negative influence on their performance of their main jobs. It bears repeating that what an employee does on his own time is generally his own business, but that a company can legitimately concern itself with the off-premises activities if they are detrimental to its interest.

The Tribune Publishing Company was ruled to have just cause for discharging its *Oakland Tribune* drama critic, who accepted outside work as a press agent for the operator of a summer theater. The arbiter agreed with the employer's contention that the outside employment created a conflict of interest. Further, it violated a contract provision that "Without permission in writing from the Publisher, no employee shall use the name of the Publisher or his connection with the Publisher or any featured title or other material of the Publisher to exploit in any way his outside endeavor." The critic never obtained the employer's permission to act as a press agent; she did get the job through her connection with the publisher; and she allowed her name, which was also the name of her column, to be used in promoting the summer theater.[105]

An employee at the Forest City Foundries Company asked to leave work early because he was "sleepy, tired, and sick." The Foreman denied the request because he did not consider fatigue an adequate excuse. An argument ensued, during which the employee threatened to hit the foreman. Later that same day, after management discussions, a termination record was signed and shown to the employee's steward, and the employee was then sent a telegram notifying him of the discharge. He filed a grievance, and it came out in the hearings that he had been working for someone else part time. The arbitrator commented:

> In the instant case the Arbitrator has concluded that the Company was justified in discharging the Grievant. Grievant had the benefit of both vigorous and conscientious defense by his Union representatives and considerate suggestions and discussions from the Company personnel director. However, his extensive moonlighting has apparently taken its toll both physically and emotionally, rendering him overly sensitive to the supervisory efforts of his Foreman and others. It is unfortunate that in an age when most workers are actively seeking constantly shorter workweeks, this Grievant found it necessary to work at a second job for "between 6 and 39 hours per week." During the week of the discharge, the Grievant worked at his second job 34 hours. It is not the responsibility of the primary Employer to absorb intemperate conduct caused by fatigue or illness brought on by moonlighting activities.[106]

Presumably the company would not have challenged the secondary work if it had not had a negative effect on the grievant's performance, attendance, and attitude. The secondary employer was not a competitor.

There are circumstances under which a person has been held to be entitled to take a job with a secondary employer when he was physically unable to work for a primary employer. For example, an employee injured his arm while working at a cemetery, and could no longer do the only type of work available for him there. During the period of his idleness, he was able to take a job as a bartender because the pains in his arm, for which he later underwent an operation, did not interfere with these lighter duties. When the cemetery management discovered him working at his second job, it discharged him, only to have Arbitrator Robert L. Stutz subsequently reinstate him.

A firm that supplied janitorial services to offices discharged an employee for performing similar tasks in a tavern after completing his work for the primary employer. The arbiter ruled that the discharge was not for just or proper cause. First of all, the company had no rule or established past practice prohibiting dual employment. Second, the tavern keeper was not a competitor, nor did the employee's duties involve any trade secrets or even semiskilled work. Third, though the company had complained of the quality of his work, these complaints were not related in any way to the fact that he had the other job. The arbitrator reinstated him with full seniority and back pay.[107]

Strikes

Employees who engage in an economic strike can be replaced by the company with impunity. In contrast, those who engage in an unfair labor practice strike must be reinstated. In fact, jobs must be made for them if need be, even if hired replacements have to be dismissed.

The *Labor Relations Expediter* of the Bureau of National Affairs provides an excellent description of strikes. It calls them organized labor's major weapon in fighting for its aim when private negotiation, conciliation, mediation, arbitration, and the orders of government agencies have failed to produce a resolution of employer-union differences. The national labor policy of the United States as set forth in the LMRA is based on the right of employees to strike in concert if collective negotiations fail to provide them with what they deem satisfactory in wages, hours, and working conditions.

In response to the strike weapon in an economic dispute, the employer may attempt to keep his operations going by hiring replacements for strikers. He also may put the terms that were spurned by the union into effect after a genuine impasse has been reached. Or he may anticipate a strike threat by laying off his workers.

As has been observed several times, there is little question regarding a company's right to discipline and discharge workers for violating a no-strike pledge in the labor agreement. Customarily the issue before the arbitrator in disputes over company action against strikers is whether the employer was arbitrary or discriminatory in his selection of those to be disciplined or discharged. Arbiters have usually ruled that a company cannot single out an individual striker for discipline or for heavier punishment unless it can prove that he demonstrated leadership of the strike.

When union officials have participated in such unlawful activity, a harsher penalty will generally be upheld on the premise that this is a graver offense for them than for the ordinary employee. Not only must union officials refrain from engaging in "negative leadership"; some arbiters hold that they have an obligation, by virtue of their union position, to demonstrate "affirmative leadership" in opposition to any contractual violations by employees.

Whether participation in a wildcat strike justifies the company's denying strikers all the protective provisions of the contract is an un-settled question among arbitrators. Some practitioners have ruled that workers have terminated their service under the contract by participating in an illegal strike. One concluded that violation of the no-strike article did not terminate the contract and that participants did not cease to be employees. Another arbiter held that an employer was free to ignore the seniority and recall provisions of the contract when resuming operations after a strike when no claim was made that the recall process adopted was discriminatory.

Arbitrators are nearly unanimous in holding that employees who engage in misconduct during a strike, whether a legal or an illegal work stoppage, are properly subject to discipline or discharge. The offenses often occur in connection with management's exercise of its legal right to continue to operate its enterprise during a strike. More often than not, they consist of violence, threats, and intimidation perpetrated against workers who continue to enter the employer's premises during the strike and perform their jobs, which is also a legal right.

Arbitrator J. Fred Holly discussed the labor practitioner's respon-sibility in cases like this to determine what penalty should be considered appropriate to the crime:

> A strike situation embraces an environment vastly different [from] that which exists in the daily relations of the parties. Generally, the workaday principle that discharge is for just cause if it is not arbitrary, capricious or discriminatory has obvious shortcomings when applied to employees' action during strikes. In the latter situation there is an absence of super-vision; the atmosphere is emotionally charged, particularly if the Employer exercises his right to keep the plant open; there is a more ready availability of remedies at law; community attitudes and pressures bring an added force to bear on the parties; and all of these factors are in-creased in intensity in a first strike situation such as the subject one. As a consequence, acts of indiscretion and violence are to be more expected during strikes. Yet, the expectation of incidents of violence does not remove the need for or the right to discipline. Violence is not to be con-doned except under the most unusual circumstances. Given the aforementioned differences, however, disciplinary action short of discharge may be required in a strike situation, even though a similar act might warrant discharge in a normal work situation. Therefore, it is in-cumbent upon the Arbitrator to examine all circumstances that exist in the strike situation before deciding upon the propriety of the discipline administered.[108]

The Westinghouse Electric Corporation satisfied the arbiter of a dispute arising out of a wildcat strike that its discipline, which was "short of discharge," was appropriate. The strike began when employees failed to return to work after the lunch break. Pickets appeared at the plant gates about 2:00 P.M., and on the following morning all entrances to the plant were barricaded. An employee who normally reported to work about 2:45 P.M. came in early, at 1:30, to recover some insurance due him. He had no knowledge that pickets were at the gates since he was inside the plant at the time the picket lines formed. He reported to his regular job, noting only that several of his fellow employees were absent. When he left the plant in his car at 11:45 that evening, a black sedan started to follow him. The sedan tried to pull alongside, first on one side and then on the other. When it finally succeeded in doing so, its occupants threw several rocks or heavy objects at the right side of his car, at least two of them striking and breaking the glass in two windows. There was sufficient light from street lamps for the worker to identify the people in the sedan.

After he reported the incident to a supervisor, one of the offending employees was given a 10-day disciplinary suspension and two others were each given a five-day suspension. Arbitrator Al T. Singletary upheld the company's action.[109]

At the General American Transportation Corporation, management imposed three-day disciplinary suspensions on 18 of 45 employees who engaged in a strike in violation of the contract. Arbitrator Harry Abrahams ruled that the discipline was not discriminatory since the 18 employees either picketed the plant or were union officers who acted as spokesmen for the strikers. The 27 workers who were exempted were not on the picket line and did not actively participate in keeping the employees out on strike. The arbitrator considered that the company in this matter was very lenient as it had authority under the contract to impose the discharge penalty but instead chose to exact only a three-day suspension.[110]

The misconduct of employees during an economic strike at a hospital took the form of sitdowns in the hospital administrator's office. This activity willfully violated a state court order prohibiting strikers from trespassing on hospital premises. Moreover, it was designed to force the hospital to recognize a union that had been unable to establish its majority status before the state court. The company discharged the participants.

The doctrine of the NLRB in a case involving Fansteel, Inc., was of interest to the arbiter in this connection. At Fansteel, a group of employees seized and held two key buildings. The Supreme Court of the United States supported the discharge of the employees, stating: "We are unable to conclude that Congress intended to compel employers to retain persons in their employ regardless of their unlawful conduct" or "to invest those who go on strike with an immunity from discharge for acts of trespass...."[111] A comment of the arbitrator in the hospital dispute is instructive: "Violence is implicit in the very act of sitting down; no matter that there is no additional violence committed in its execution." The arbiter held that those engaged in the sitdown were guilty of serious misconduct and should be disciplined.[112]

The opinion of an arbitrator in a General Electric Company case is perhaps unique and certainly representative of a minority viewpoint. In this dispute, the company imposed disciplinary suspensions on three union members for picket line misconduct during an economic strike. The arbiter held that the employer's actions were not for just cause because in his opinion the company's right to exercise its disciplinary function was operative only during the time the employee was obligated to contribute to production. Since an economic strike was in progress, the workers were therefore freed of this obligation. It was also significant to him that the company had kept its plant gates open and operated its business during the work stoppage. In this connection he commented:

> Under the circumstances, the Company's right to discipline employees engaged in an illegal strike where it itself is a contributor to a violence-provoking environment can only be judged against the same criteria that are invoked by any citizen who takes measures to defend his property in a civil disturbance. The criteria of judgment expected are much more vigorous than in ordinary cases of alleged employee misbehavior under normal conditions.[113]

The arbiter concluded that the three disciplined employees should be reinstated with full back pay.

Holdings such as this are rare, and this seems fortunate. It is regrettable that when a company exercises its legal right to operate its business or an employee his right to pursue his livelihood, some perceive such a justifiable act as irresponsible and unreasonably provocative of the illegal conduct of others.

5. Union Officials —
Discipline and Discharge

The most delicate type of discharge or discipline case is one that finds a union official the target of management's action.

The dual role of local union officer, as an employee, and also as an official of a labor organization, gives an added dimension to his conduct which is not shared by ordinary employees. In the role of employee, he has the rights and privileges of other rank-and-file employees within his bargaining unit, and he is governed by the rules and regulations which apply to his co-workers. While in his job as an employee of the company, the requirements of attendance, punctuality, quality, production output, and the like are the same for him as they would be for any other employee of the company. But while operating in his capacity of union representative, he enjoys a certain latitude and freedom in his day-to-day application, administration, and implementation of the union contract. As a union representative, he becomes co-equal with the company's supervisors, thus enabling him to represent and advocate the positions and interests of his constituents.

Management's discipline or discharge of a union official frequently raises the questions: Is the motivation for its action union animus or discrimination? Was the union representative's act performed during a time when he was operating in his role as an employee, or was he acting as a union official and, therefore, by reason of this representational cloak, entitled to some special consideration or immunity?

This chapter will describe some representative cases dealing with the punishment of union officials for on-the-job rules violations while acting in their dual role of employee and union official. To enable the supervisor to better see the several principles involved, various arbitrator's decisions are reviewed for supporting authority, and to show how the issues raised by such cases are commonly dealt with.

Insubordination

In cases involving alleged insubordination by individuals who hold the office of union steward, the penalties are generally the same as for rank-and-file employees if the steward was insubordinate as an employee.

In one such case, at the Dominion Electric Co. where a union official refused a job assignment related to his particular tasks as an employee, the arbitrator concluded that the company did not discharge him with intent to discriminate but rather for his refusal as an employee to carry out a proper order.[114]

At the American Can Co., the employer was found justified in discharging for "gross and defiant insubordination," a union president who repeatedly left his bargaining unit job without proper supervisory leave to investigate grievances.[115]

At Chrysler Corp., under a contract which obligated the chief steward to report to his foreman the number and nature of grievances he wished to investigate, the employer was found justified in discharging the steward after his refusal to perform unit overtime work. The steward claimed he was investigating grievances (and so could not work overtime), but refused to identify them as required by contractual provision. In upholding the dismissal, the arbitrator ruled that the steward had been instructed by his foreman to report for the assignment and he had been warned to identify the specific grievances under investigation, or return to his job, or be discharged.[116]

In a case with a different twist, the arbitrator sustained the discharge of a union steward who functioned continually in the capacity of a union official outside of a fixed, agreed upon hourly period established for stewards to handle grievances and to otherwise discharge their duties. Although he was acting as a union official, his refusal to stop was in total disregard of specific contractual regulations which limited that union activity.[117]

The labor agreement's provisions are the controlling factor here. The regulations and practices under the contract determine when an employee-union representative can function as a union official, and to what extent. Absent some contract arrangement to the contrary, the general rule holds that such workers have two obligations – first to their job as an employee, and second to their capacity as a union official – and, in that particular order of priority.

But where the steward is on union business, the usual requirement of "obey first, grieve later" is most often not applied by arbiters, if the orders given are in conflict with the union's rights under the labor agreement.

In one such situation, upon dismissing the complaint, an arbiter held that:

> There is a clear distinction between the case of a supervisor telling an employee to go back to his job and supervisor telling the union to stop investigating a grievance. The company and union have met on equal terms and adopted a contract recognizing each other's right.... If he (steward) could rightly be penalized, it would put the entire grievance machinery, set up by agreement of the parties at the highest levels, at the mercy of supervisors with the possibility of great harm to the relations of the parties, even to a complete breakdown of the grievance machinery.[118]

A new and different type of remedy was rendered by another arbitrator. Where a union committeeman was discharged for refusing to perform assigned work which he believed was not covered by his classification, the arbitrator concluded that the committeeman's trouble was due to overzealousness in his union office. He reinstated the committeeman without back pay upon the condition he resign from office as union committeeman and pledge to remain out of such office.[119]

Gambling, Dishonesty and Drinking

Insubordination is not the only offense for which union representatives may find themselves subjected to discipline. All plant rules and other regulatory conditions which govern employee behavior are also applicable to local union representatives in equal measure while in their capacity of employee. Union officials have found themselves in serious trouble with management for their transgressions in a number of areas. For example, the discharge of a union steward was found to be a warranted exercise of managerial discretion when the company established that the steward (as an employee) was guilty of submitting false piecework tickets, thus claiming additional compensation for work which he was unable to prove he had performed.[120]

When a union president was discharged for excessive absenteeism, the question was asked: Where is the proper balance between the latitude provided him in his capacity as union president and his obligations as an employee? In examining this situation, the arbitrator said:

> The grievant was out an inordinate number of days for a variety of reasons: outside union business, illness, personal reasons. He was warned repeatedly about this, even to the extent of being given a

disciplinary layoff. . . . Knowing that the company took a serious view of his absences and his leaving the job without first securing permission, he made little effort after the disciplinary layoff, to comply with the reasonable requirements expected of him, but continued to absent himself on union business, aware on the basis of his previous record, that the chances were good that he might also be out for illness. Under these circumstances, I consider the company has justified its charge of excessive absenteeism. The grievance is denied.[121]

In the case above, there was a mixture of absences for illness and personal reasons, and others for purposes of engaging in union business.

By no means is there unanimity of arbitral opinion on this point. A representative case of their disagreement is one in which the arbitrator ruled that the employer was not justified in discharging a union president for chronic absenteeism and tardiness, in accordance with the plant rules, even though the president had received prior warnings regarding the excessive number of his unreported absences. The arbitral premise here was that the majority of absences and occasions of tradiness apparently were necessitated by legitimate union business, and the remaining number of absences were not sufficient to constitute chronic absenteeism.

Here again we see that distinction drawn between duties and functions as an employee, as contrasted with the second part of the dual role, the activities and responsibilities as a union representative.

Union officials have also been disciplined for gambling on company time and on company premises. Under a plant rule providing for immediate discharge of "any employee drinking or gambling on the company property," an employer was found justified in discharging a local union officer who had been operating baseball and number pools at work. In upholding the discharge, the arbitrator said:

> Patently the issue here is whether the grievant was discharged for just cause or if, as the union charges, the dismissal was capricious and discriminatory. The company avers the discipline meted out was just and proper because: (1) all four types of gambling games conducted by the grievant violated the criminal code and had they adopted a laissez-faire policy and closed their eyes to such violations they could have been ejected from their premises by the very terms of the lease agreement; (2) rule 6 of the company rules and regulations provides immediate dismissal for gambling; and (3) the gambling activities conducted by the grievant adversely affected plant productivity as is evidenced by substantial productivity improvement after the grievant's discharge and the gambling ceased.[122]

Here again, the employee-union official violated a plant rule while acting in the capacity of employee. His union office did not cloak him in immunity.

Falsification of the employment application of a newly elected union officer was reason for yet another discharge. While the officer was militant and aggressive, and his discharge followed by one day the union's strike vote over grievances he had been processing, the arbitrator found that the employer's action was not discriminatory premised on the employee's union activities. In his decision, he commented:

> Whether or not he had been a union official his falsification would have supported discharge. That he was a union official would not mitigate against the impropriety of what he had done. . . . The grievance dismissed.[123]

Again, consequential to the arbitral findings was the absence of any discrimination or union animus on the part of the employer.

The discharge of two union officials who drank on the job on company premises on Christmas Eve was sustained by an arbitrator who ruled that drinking on the job was dangerous to the employee and to his fellow workers. In this case, it was also a direct violation of the contract. Despite a union argument that both men were officers of the local and that the company had failed to detect other employees guilty of the same offense, he ruled that these considerations were immaterial and sustained the company's discharge action.[124]

In still another interesting, insightful case involving violation of plant rules and regulations, a union president was discharged for (1) preparing an order which directed the removal of exterior plant floodlights, (2) forging a plant superintendent's signature on the order, and (3) filing the form as a legitimate order. It proved of no consequence when the union president-employee alleged that he merely wanted to play a joke on a night watchman, since in the arbitrator's view the faked order might have resulted in loss of company property by fire or theft, thus making this a serious offense. In commenting about the affect of a union president's discharge on the relationship between the parties, the arbitrator said:

> It was contended on the part of the union that L_____ had been a longtime faithful and competent employee of the company and that he had been a union member from the time that the union had first been recognized by the company, and was, in effect, president of the union at the time of his discharge, and was also chairman of the negotiating

committee dealing directly with the company for the renewal of the contract at the time of his discharge.

If laxity to the extent of permitting the subscription of that of a
superintendent's name to an order affecting the company's property is to
be permitted to the president of a union, the example set for the general
workers in the plant is not conducive to sound labor-management relationship and mutual respect in their varied dealings.[125]

Here we have a case containing an additional complicating
ingredient — the company's action was taken during the time that
bargaining was in progress for a renewed labor agreement, with the
union president a key participant. But that fact notwithstanding, the
company's action (1) showed no union animus; (2) there was no other
aspect of discrimination; (3) the company met a test of bearing the
burden of proof; and (4) it met a standard of just cause. This was then
sufficient to overcome the problem of the event occurring during the
period of collective bargaining, and those suspicions attendant therefore.

Ignorance of the Law

It is common for arbitrators to weigh the length of time a union
official has been in office and thereby consider his degree of sophistication and familiarity with the scope and responsibilities of his union
authority when reviewing any punishment of the official. Arbitral opinion often holds that a new or inexperienced steward's improprieties in
office may be excused, or partially justified by the fact that he is not com-
pletely informed. Such was the story in a case when a union committeeman was disciplined for violating a company rule forbidding distribution of handbills on company property. The committeeman had acted
in the honest belief he was within his rights because of a recent NLRB
decision involving a different company, which found illegal the company
order prohibiting distribution of union leaflets on company parking lots.

Another arbitrator went a large step further in resolving a dispute
over a discharged steward who, on his first day in office, told his foreman
he was entitled to go where he pleased and proceeded to "roam" up and
down, in disregard of his foreman's repeated orders. Although the arbitrator fully censured the behavior of this steward, he reasoned that:

[The steward] would nevertheless have taken immediate proper direction
from his own chief within the union, the divisional steward. However,
this opportunity to give the inexperienced steward timely correction was
ignored by the foreman. The green steward was given a further oppor-

tunity to repeat his mistake and to sink further into the consequences of his blunder.... Modern personnel relations require from both sides and their representatives at least a reasonable degree of sympathetic tolerance. On the night of the dispute, S_____ was an inexperienced, newly appointed steward. Management appears to have been guilty almost of entrapment of the steward into a harsh consequence of an ignorant mistake, instead of cooperating in a charitable and tolerant effort to correct his erroneous assumptions.[126]

Although most arbiters will not go quite so far as this, generally speaking, the majority give ample consideration to the factor of inexperience in union officials. An arbitrator who joined this majority reinstated discharged union officers even though evidence established that they had instigated and participated in a strike in violation of the contract. This arbitrator also considered the inexperience of the union officials, the newness of the employer's operations, the local union and the labor contract; as well as the accumulation of grievances which had led to employees' unrest, all to be mitigating factors in this case.[127]

The best course of action for a supervisor therefore is to (1) give the erring new union official a thorough counseling on the breadth and limits of his union freedom and responsibility before any disciplinary action is deemed applicable; (2) give him a warning and a second chance to correct his improper conduct before action is taken; and (3) advise higher union officials of the complications experienced and solicit their cooperation and higher authority to get the right message across to their inexperienced brethren.

Countermanding Management's Orders

For the most part, there does appear to be unanimity of opinion among arbitrators about the impropriety of the union countermanding management's orders, so long as the order deals with matters generally falling within management's domain. Harry Shulman, respected spokesman and statesman in the arbitration process and former umpire with the Ford Motor Co. and the United Auto Workers, articulated this philosophy in one of his many cases when he said:

No committeeman or other union officer is entitled to instruct employees to disobey supervision's orders *no matter how strongly* he may believe that the orders are in violation of the agreement. If he believes that an improper order has been issued, his course is to take the matter up with supervision and to seek to effect an adjustment. Failing to effect an adjustment, he may file a grievance. But he may *not* tell the employee to disregard the order.[128] (Emphasis added.)

The overwhelming weight of majority opinion in arbitral circles reflects the view that an industrial plant is not a debating society. When controversies arise, as they inevitably will, the operation of the enterprise must go on while the dispute is being discussed and resolved. The authority for directing that it go on is vested solely in supervision. The grievance procedure is designed to adequately recompense employees for any abuse of authority by supervision. But the remedy under the labor agreement for violations of rights lies in the grievance and arbitration provisions.

For the union representative, or the individual employee, to disregard or countermand supervision's orders is to replace the grievance with the extracontractual method of individual determination and action, and such must be the advice of a union representative to his constituents. The only exception to this is orders which would require the employee to perform a criminal or unlawful or immoral act. Also in this category are supervisor's directives which if carried out would jeopardize the health, safety or welfare of the employees. But if the management order falls within its proper boundaries, the union representative's posture should be that the employee is obliged to obey the supervisor's instructions and to seek redress and correction through the grievance procedures. The efficient and orderly operation of a plant requires that employees and union representatives alike respect the authority of their supervisors. Union representatives who advise employees to circumvent or disobey reasonable instructions issued by the company open themselves to possible disciplinary action.

Union Official's Responsibility

Generally, arbitrators hold that local officials not only have similar responsibility as other employees with regard to performance of their regular jobs, but also carry an additional burden, as union officials, of enforcing the contract, and influencing other employees to comply with its terms. For example, where a union official participates in an unauthorized work stoppage, his offense is graver than that of the other participating employees.

This principle was voiced in a situation where the employer imposed a suspension against a shop steward for engaging in a strike in violation of the labor agreement. In his award, the arbiter said:

The proposition that affirmative obligations of leadership in upholding the grievance procedure and opposing work stoppages devolved upon an employee, who by reason of seniority and status as a union officer must be held to have achieved a position of influence, has hitherto found acceptance under this and other agreements. Implicit in it is the thought that if those prominent and influential in the affairs of the union fail to so support the vital provisions of the agreement, the parties' expectations that they will be complied with during the life of the agreement become altogether illusory.[129]

Some arbitrators have even viewed a union official's passive behavior in the face of known employee violations of the contract as a type of "negative leadership." This general principle of "negative vs. affirmative leadership" is one shared by many arbiters. One such opinion was expressed in a case where the local union president, union committeeman, and shop steward were disciplined for failing to prevent an unauthorized work stoppage.

Local union officials are the spokesmen for the workers. They are their leaders. They, therefore, have responsibilities *over and beyond* those of the rank and file. Local union officials are *obligated aggressively to oppose actions* that violate commitments undertaken in good faith. Local union officials are bound by virtue of their office to set personal examples of opposition to contract violation. *They cannot be passive; they must vigorously seek to prevent contract violations by their constituents.*[130] (Emphasis added.)

Although this view is shared by the great majority of arbitrators, a few dissenting voices are occasionally still heard. Supervisors should also be aware of these minority opinions as well, and not be deluded by a belief there is total unanimity. Typical of such minority opinions was a decision where the employer was ruled to be not justified in discharging a union committeeman who had participated in a wildcat strike, since the committeeman had neither incited nor led the strike, and no other employee who participated in the strike was penalized. The arbitrator held that the fact the discharged employee was a union officer did not warrant a greater penalty than that imposed on other employees. The arbitral position here was that the responsibility of committeemen as union officers was not to the employer but to other employees and the union. No further comment will be made on this type of holding. Suffice it to say that this does represent the minority view on the principle of negative vs. affirmative leadership.

Union officials also have been held answerable for their personal behavior in carrying out union duties. Despite the relaxed and loose usage of shop vernacular, arbiters have upheld discharge of stewards for verbally insulting and intimidating members of management. Whether the remarks exceed the typical and normal shop vernacular of the particular institution, and are threatening, insulting and intimidating are factors in what the ultimate arbitral determination may be. Also, it may be relevant if the behavior is such as to threaten the dignity of the supervisor and his office in the eyes of other employees, and bring this into disrepute, impinging upon his image as an authority figure.

On the other hand, an employer was not sustained in his attempt to discharge a union official who personally instigated the filing of a large number of grievances.

Employees may go only so far in demonstrating their dislike of a supervisor. But when that employee is also a union representative, his conduct and behavior should be somewhat different from that of the other employees. This was the view of one arbitrator who upheld the discharge of a union steward. Following his demotion from a job in the plant, the steward filed several grievances contending the demotion was punitive; he later filed a grievance alleging that his supervisor cursed the men, was discriminatory, and was unfit to be a boss, which action finally resulted in his discharge. The arbitrator, in examining all the facts of the case, decided that here was more than a mere overzealous steward. Here was an individual whose combination of behavior patterns exceeded the reasonable limitations of a steward's conduct in a plant. In rendering this award, he stated that mere zealousness or militancy could not justify management discipline. But repeated and unfounded written accusations of a criminal or semicriminal nature against management personnel, threats of physical violence in retaliation, and public bullying tactics could not be condoned by upholding his grievance. Doing so would place some degree of approval on a pattern of behavior which would place the plant's collective bargaining relationship at the level of the jungle. In a somewhat similar affair, the company was found to be justified in discharging a union chief steward for filing a grievance in which he falsely charged a supervisor with manhandling another employee, a story fabricated out of whole cloth.

The discharge of a union steward who had received many prior warnings for violating a contract ban on unauthorized union activities during working hours was sustained when he again took working time on union matters which should have been handled by the union's financial secretary in accordance with an established and satisfactory procedure. In discussing the steward's misconduct, the arbitrator said the steward

> was guilty of a serious disservice to his fellow workers, in that he needlessly gave rise to irritation and friction which especially, if

repeated, must inevitably result in injury to the morale and productive efficiency of the plant, as well as to good labor-management relations.

It cannot be pointed out too often that the position of a steward is an important and honorable one, and that the individual filling the office should be a person who, while fully carrying out the important responsibilities of his office, and protecting the rights of his fellow workers, is nevertheless able to retain the respect and goodwill of management by the exercise not merely of zeal alone, but also of good common sense.[131]

By virtue of his office, a union representative has a special obligation to observe and respect the collective bargaining agreement. He is duty bound to protect employees in the grievance procedure against violations of the agreement by management. The agreement gives him special rights and privileges in order that he may perform that function. He cannot with impunity turn his back on the very agreement which it is his duty to defend.

A union steward is also a leader; indeed, it is reasonable to assume that it is also because he is a leader that he acquires his union office. It follows then that when a steward participates in a work stoppage, making no effort to police that contract violation as he does others, or bring it to a close, he sets an example for the other employees and indicates by his action that the stoppage has his tacit approval and sanction. This is a graver offense than participation by an ordinary employee and may justify a more serious penalty.

Arbitral Standards

Although parties to labor agreements have achieved, and enjoy today, a higher level of sophistication than at any time in the past 25 years, cases involving discharge and discipline for union activities are still a too frequent issue in arbitration. An analysis of the many hundreds of published cases on these subjects may lead one to various conclusions. The parties still have a long way to go before they have achieved a desirable level of understanding of the rights and responsibilities incumbent on each, and also those possessed by the other. Perhaps, at least in part, this reflects the failure of both parties to assume their proper responsibility to develop, train, and instruct their respective representatives as to the proper role of each. Perhaps it also reflects a failure of the parties to realize that each is here to stay, that each is entitled to its respective needs, positions, principles and philosophies, and that the only road to a peaceful and constructive relationship lies down the path of mutual acceptance, respect and understanding.

But laying this aside and examining only the manner generally speaking, in which most arbitrators view such disputes, arbitrators concur in their views regarding the bounds of union authority and the degree of behavioral freedom of the union representative. They impose the same criterion of just cause where disciplinary action is taken against the steward for alleged misconduct as an employee. When a union claim is made of anti-union discrimination in the absence of conclusive evidence of this, the burden of proof to support this claim falls on the union. But in judging such cases certain arbitral standards are used.

1. What has been the relationship between the parties? What is generally the atmosphere between the company organization and union as an institution? And, what has been the acting management representatives' relationship with the particular union representative being disciplined?

2. Is there any evidence of discrimination or union animus? Has the disciplined steward been a troublesome, aggressive, militant individual—perhaps one who has filed many grievances or abused paid union time provisions of the agreement? If there is any evidence of union animus, the burden of disproving it will fall on the employer.

3. Was there in fact a proven violation; did the steward commit the offense of which he is accused; and can the company meet fully its burden of proof?

4. What has been the company's disciplinary treatment of other employees who are not union representatives, for similar offenses where the circumstances were similar and related to this case?

5. Was the union representative's conduct provoked, and did management's representative also engage in similar conduct; threats, name calling, intimidation, and so forth?

6. Did the incident, if provocative and inflammatory, occur in the presence of other employees, or did it happen in the privacy of a meeting between the principals only? And were the remarks and the behavior well beyond the customary shop vernacular and mode of conduct— customary in this context, meaning that which is typical, accepted and routine in this particular plant's day-to-day climate and atmosphere?

7. And, was the union representative being disciplined new to his office, recently elected or appointed, with a small amount of experience and understanding of his proper role and responsibilities? Or, was he a knowledgeable and informed individual, with considerable experience and understanding of his duties, his rights, and his obligations?

A management sensitive to the above criteria, which gives full consideration and weight to each of these factors that may be applicable in any particular case, should find itself better equipped to defend its action and have it sustained or supported by the arbitrator—the only person who, in the final analysis, sits in a position to overturn a management decision.

The final answer to diminishing such problems rests in a realization by each party of the rights of the other. If the number of such cases is to be reduced to a realistic level, indicative of mutual respect and understanding, each must assume its educational and informational responsibilities and create an industrial climate wherein there is, in fact, joint respect, understanding and cooperation.

Management has agreed in the labor agreement that when carrying out its responsibilities, it will follow certain procedures or take into account specified factors involving the equities of employees. In such situations, management's failures to perform the particular responsibility in the manner agreed upon is subject to challenge in the grievance procedure which may be subject to appeal to arbitration.

Moreover, even with regard to managerial rights not in any way regulated or limited by a labor agreement, management should act wisely and justly. The arbitrary and inconsiderate use of power is a sure invitation to ultimate limitation of that power. In union-management relations, management's injudicious use of its rights and responsibilities affords the union ammunition for demanding further contractual limitations on management in future negotiations.

6. The Conflicting Needs
of the Three Parties

The labor agreement represents the compromise of the legitimate needs of three parties — the company, the employees and the union. Each of the parties approaches the bargaining table in possession of certain basic needs which they hope to have gratified there. The problem is that certain of these wants and needs bring the parties into some degree of conflict. This has to be so since the satisfaction of one party's needs by the other can often result in the granting party ultimately receiving less than it might otherwise want and need in satisfaction of its own needs. The point is that these differing and contradictory needs between the parties produce basic differences of viewpoint, and therefore some amount of conflict is an integral part of the relationship between the three parties and is sometimes unavoidable.

First, the most basic and essential needs of each of the three parties have been listed below for review. This will be followed by an examination of each and how they interact and produce some conflict between the parties.

Employee Needs	*Union Needs*	*Management Needs*
1. Sense of Belonging	1. "More" — perpetuate itself	1. To make a profit
2. Respect and dignity	2. To increase membership	2. To compete
3. Security in jobs and job skills	3. To improve its economic status	3. To direct and fully utilize its work force — less employees
4. Opportunity for advancement	4. To be competitive	4. Maintain discipline and efficiency
5. To advance economically		

Briefly reviewing a number of the above, and the manner in which they come into conflict with certain other needs of the other parties, it will be noted that among the employees' needs are those to have a security in their jobs and job skills, opportunities for advancement, and the ability to advance economically. These are all legitimate and understandable needs and to the extent that the particular company is able to satisfy them, its employees will probably be more satisfactory and productive. However, if these particular employee needs are wholly satisfied, they inevitably diminish the gratification of certain company needs. For example, among management's needs is the desire to be able to direct and fully utilize its work force, operating its plant in as economical and efficient a manner as possible. The objective, of course, is to be competitive and make a profit. To accomplish this end, the company frequently endeavors to reduce or remove labor content from jobs, having them become, to a greater extent, machine-controlled operations or automated through technological advance. This is also a legitimate and understandable need and objective of the company. The problem it raises is that in so doing, management threatens the security of employees in their total employment relationship and it clearly results in a devaluation of their jobs resulting in tasks of lesser worth and jobs requiring lesser skills and employee ability.

On the one hand you have employees with a legitimate need for security in their jobs and job skills, on the other hand the company needs to direct and fully utilize its work force and obtain the maximum work output attainable with as few employees as possible. These objectives are contradictory and in opposition. Intertwined in this conflict is the union with an objective to increase membership. The consequence of conflict is predictable. If the company is successful in meeting its objectives, numbers of jobs are reduced, employee security is threatened, union membership decreases. As mentioned before, if labor content in jobs is reduced, the remaining job portion may well be of lesser wage value and employee job skills are consequently eroded. The union's failure to prevent this company accomplishment may operate to put it in jeopardy competitively between this group of employees and another union. For the union to cooperate with the company in this endeavor will almost certainly cause it to fall into disrepute with its members.

However, if the union and the employees are successful in harnessing or throttling the company's efforts in this connection, the company's ability to compete and make a profit may be seriously threatened or even impaired.

The most prominent example of such conflict between parties comes when you compare the employees' need to advance economically with the company's need to make a profit. Obviously the employees' economic advancement comes purely from management's revenues which come from profit. To the extent that management enables the employees to advance economically, it diminishes its profits. To the extent it denies or does not give full consideration to the employees' need to advance economically, it enhances its profit. Therefore, the question over which the parties will always have conflict is that of, "how much is too much, and how much would be just enough," for each party. Some degree of conflict, at least between the company and its employees, is inevitable. The inevitability of such conflict between the company and the union is even more apparent. As a political organization, the union must always be striving for more and it must be striving for more even when it does not actually expect to achieve it. The mere act of doing so, and vigorously representing the interests of the employees, enhances its stature with the employees. Of course, the union must also be occasionally achieving more for the employees. Only in this way can the union perpetuate itself as the employee's representatives. It goes without saying, its target for acquiring more is always the company. And, to the extent the company satisfies the union's needs in these areas, it diminishes its own profitability, or its own ability to direct and utilize its working force.

The lifeblood of the union is union dues. The greater number of members, the more profitable and economically adequate is the union. The usual objective of the company is to reduce the number of employees it needs—reducing as much labor content as possible from jobs—since the cost of labor content is customarily the most expensive factor in the operation of the company's business. However, this objective brings it into conflict with the union, whose objective is to increase membership, which is threatened when there are diminishing numbers of employees.

Conflicts between union and company frequently arise over the activities of employee-union representatives elected to function in the plant. These department stewards, grievance chairman, local union committeemen, vice-presidents, presidents, etc., naturally consider themselves the policemen of the contract, charged with responsibility to ensure its enforcement and guard against its being violated. The best time for them to conduct their policing activities is during working hours. Usually they expect the employer to continue to pay them for such activities engaged in during working hours. Whether paid or not, the potential for conflict is intrinsic in their situation. While on union business, they are not engaged in productive effort on their own job, nor, from the company's point of view, are they engaged in an activity which may be deemed productive in any sense of the word. They may be interrupting other employees from their productive tasks. They may be engaged with management people, which interrupts them from their given tasks. If they exceed a period of time considered sufficient by the company for them to accomplish their union activity during working hours, a dispute will follow when the company attempts to curtail it. The reason for such disputes is obvious—the management path to the satisfaction of some of its legitimate objectives and needs is on a collision course with the union's path toward the satisfaction of some of its legitimate objectives and needs.

Oftentimes all three of the parties are in conflict, one with the other. An example of this occurs when management reduces the worth of a given job by some type of mechanization which requires less employee skill to perform it. This reduction in skill requirement results in a job which management will desire to pay less for, a consequence certainly not in tune with the employees' desires. The employees then turn to the union for defense against this action, bringing the union into conflict with the company. Then, if the union is unable to accomplish for the employees that which they seek, it is failing to represent the employees as adequately as the union feels it should be, and its security as employee representatives is threatened. If the union agrees with the company, conflict will result between it and its own members.

These are just a few of the factors which foremen should be cognizant of in their relationships with their employees and union representatives. Too many supervisors view the receipt of a grievance as a personal affront, without realizing that some controversies of the type described have always been, and probably always will be, an inherent part of the relationship of the three parties. A better understanding of these needs, drives and motivations will enable foremen to more logically and intelligently handle employee complaints.

Too many management people are idealistic and consequently unrealistic in their expectations. They may sincerely believe that a friction-free relationship is achievable. They may seriously think that a foreman is failing in his job if he is receiving grievances from workers. This is not to infer that such is impossible. It is to say, on the other hand, that grievances in and of themselves are not necessarily bad, nor indicative of a poor employer-employee relationship. Also, in the community of people who form the bargaining unit there resides a whole community of individual interests and needs, both commonly shared as well as divergent, from one to the other. Many of these needs and interests are predictably going to be different from those of the company's, which comprise its institutional needs and interests. Grievances are going to result. Grievances are not necessarily bad. As a matter of fact, they are the instrument of the contractual procedure which enables employees to communicate with the employer while work goes on. They are a safety valve, a means for giving off steam before things get to volatile proportions, and a way for workers to let the company know what's on their mind.

If looked at positively by the company, grievances can be considered in a beneficial light. They enable employees to get complaints off their chests rather than have them fester and create larger difficulties.

They allow the company to correct mistakes it makes. They are another channel of communication upward. They provide the company with another channel downward. They allow work to go on peacefully without interruption while problems are solved. They may reveal contractual shortcomings and highlight real or potential problem areas. They build a body of common law with precedent value which enables the foreman to treat employees in future, like situations equally.

To overcome or neutralize some of the areas of conflicting needs, there are certain avenues open to the interested employer. In recognition of their people-assets, organizations with modern employee relations policies and attitudes have found it wise and expedient to consider employees a part of the picture in every major decision they contemplate, and to keep them informed and reassured that their interests are always considered. An analysis of the areas in which most companies communicate with their employees shows that they talk to them about company:

- policies and objectives
- prospects
- products and services
- history
- plans and programs
- organization
- progress
- financial matters

- matters of institutional interests and importance
- reasons for certain decisions and actions
- changes – (contemplated and already made)
- competitors and competition

The majority of employers feel that it is desirable to disseminate this type of information because they feel it will (1) promote a better employee understanding of the company's goals and objectives; (2) establish in employees a feeling of greater participation in the operation of the business; (3) cultivate in employees a more favorable attitude toward the company; (4) develop a greater incentive for cooperation and teamwork; (5) add to the interest of employees in their work and in the company; and (6) demonstrate to the employee that the company values him as a person and recognizes him as an asset and an essential, primary member of the relationship.

When compared with these objectives, the need to have adequate employee comprehension of the economic realities of the function of the business becomes obviously paramount.

Surveys have shown that new entrants into the labor force each year have more education, on the average, than the older, retiring workers, and they tend to have more schooling than the labor force entrants who have immediately preceded them. Because the general level of education in the United States is on the rise, and because of television, newspapers, magazines and radio, people today are information-hungry and employees are generally more information-conscious. And since employees as people have read, thought and learned more, the less content they are merely to take an order and carry it out. They are also interested in knowing the "why"—and whether the "why" makes sense to them. This is why it is a must for the supervisor to know basic economic principles, since about 90 percent of management's decisions are based on economic considerations.

However, despite the dramatically improved level of education achieved by employees, obtaining employee understanding of their personal stakes in the economic realities faced by their employer is a most difficult task of management. Those companies that have met with some success in enabling their employees to achieve better economic understanding have recognized the advisability of utilizing their supervisory force.

Supervisors who talk and act in management's interest in attempting to enlighten employees regarding the economic facts of business life will find a basic problem at the outset: the fundamental problem of defining and clarifying the word "profits." In a 1966 magazine article illustrating what mistaken ideas people have about company profits, John Z. Jennings of the Singer Company mentions a poll in which Opinion Research Corporation had asked a cross-section of Americans this question:

> Let us take all the money a corporation has left after paying for materials, supplies, rent, heat and the like. This is the money that is shared by owners and employees. What is your judgment as to the percentage of this money going to employees and the percentage going to owners?

The consensus was that 75 cents out of every dollar of this divisible income went to owners and 25 cents to employees. "But in all United States corporations on a national average basis, according to official government statistics published annually by the U.S. Dept. of Commerce," Mr. Jennings goes on to say, "employee compensation was over six times as large as net profits and over 14 times as large as dividends paid."

Even Samuel Gompers, the founder of the American Federation of Labor, stated: "Companies without profits mean workers without jobs. Remember, when the boss is in financial trouble, the worker's job isn't safe." Gompers had an understanding of the fact that under our free enterprise system, the financial interests of employees and employers are interdependent. Employees can be certain of continuing on jobs only as long as the employer is achieving enough profit to meet the costs and obligations of conducting its business. But it is equally true that how well the employer is able to realize the objective of profits is dependent, to a substantial degree, on how dedicated his employees are and how capably they perform the jobs for which they are paid.

The best form of communication about the company and the economic considerations that underlie its operations is face-to-face, giving the "employee-audience" an opportunity to participate and inquire. Foremen are uniquely situated to undertake this vital communications role, but they can't simply step into this role and perform automatically. Management has an obligation first to its supervisors to help them in certain ways by (1) preparing them to function in this role; (2) supplying them with timely and factual information which they can pass along; and (3) supporting them with other forms of complementary communication to the employees from management.

The normal interchange of information, orders, and questions between a supervisor and subordinates, in most instances, relates directly or indirectly to economic issues. For example, a question about an incentive system opens up a whole new area of costs, prices, productivity and company and employee job security. A quest for better quality is related to such issues as competition, free markets, and the right of the buyer to choose someone else's product, or perhaps not to purchase at all. The question of a second shift, or conversely, a lay-off, goes back to such economic issues as supply and demand, the capital costs of expansion versus increased use of available facilities, the relation of the individual company to the economy as a whole, and so on.

Assuming that the supervisor is empowered and equipped to disseminate economic information to employees, of what value will this be to the grievance system and generally to the collective bargaining relationship between the parties? After all, why go through such an exercise unless some objective may be realized from it. The fact is that, properly employed, communications can make a major contribution in a variety of areas, only a few of which are mentioned here:

- Explain wage rates and incentives and thereby either eliminate or reduce in number grievances in this area.
- Explain management's decisions and actions and the motivations behind them, thus reducing grievances by promoting better employee understanding and acceptance.
- Maintain and, and in some cases, even produce an increase in, employees' productivity.
- Promote employee safety consciousness.
- Reduce and eliminate waste of time, energy and materials.

• Increase employees' loyalty to the company, enlarging their understanding of their mutual dependency.

• Reduce turnover, absenteeism and lateness.

Economic education of employees is intended to give the rank-and-file the basic information they desire and require in order to properly judge management's acts and policies. Many surveys have been made of the attitudes and knowledge of the average worker, and anyone analyzing such surveys soon concludes that many are woefully uninformed on certain subjects. But the average worker is a pretty smart and shrewd fellow, particularly once he is given the full and correct facts to work on. American management has created the largest and most efficient industrial organization the world has ever known—and it was accomplished primarily by concentration of most efforts of research, technology, sales, and financing. Suddenly, industry's leaders recognize that they lost sight of certain things in the process. Now the human element is finally being given its rightful place in this scheme of things and thereby it presently looms uppermost in management's thinking. It is now understood that, more and more, the art of management inextricably involves working with and through people. Of course, other such factors as methods, machinery, money and materials are of substantial importance, but employees "as people" now get their fair share of the primary spotlight when management policies are being decided.

Company newsletters and publications, personal letters, bulletin board releases and sometimes even speeches are a few of the tools and techniques used by management to get its positions and information across to employees. To stimulate upward flow of ideas and information from employees to management, suggestion programs, opinion surveys and certain types of meetings with employees are utilized.

But alone, these techniques of communication cannot do the entire, nor the most effective job. Through the immediate supervisor, management can do its most effective job of communicating. Through him management can also best determine what employees are thinking and what their attitudes generally are: he is the one to whom the employee does talk—and can talk—most naturally, and most often. He is the single representative of management nearest the employee every day; to many employees he is the management. He is the one best positioned to supply facts which employees need—when they need them to form an opinion of management.

In a highly specialized factory it is difficult to provide the interest which the old craftsman felt in the product of his hands because it was all his own, from raw material to finished masterpiece. The modern shop, if it is one where the worker can see the whole product fabricated before his eyes, still provides an opportunity to revive some of this type of interest. For the same reason, if it is possible to move workers from job to job until they have become familiar with all operations on a particular product, it will surely add to their interest. Each job takes on meaning and significance as its relation to other operations, and to the whole product, is seen.

Likewise, a worker has more interest in his machine or in his equipment if he understands how it works, the principles of its operation, what it can do, and just as important, what it cannot do; that is, the limits of its operations. When the worker knows these things, he takes an interest in that machine, and in the contribution he makes through it. Because he feels that he understands it, he comes to identify it with himself, just as he does to the job in which he has an interest. It becomes his machine, and his job, his product, his contribution.

Knowledge of his own progress usually stimulates the learning employee's interests. Supervisors long ago discovered the value of operators' performance records as an incentive, especially when presented in graphic form. Each employee likes to beat his own record, to see himself grow in skill, and often to engage in rivalry with others. Rivalry in output, however, is a form of stimulation which has to be handled wisely, especially during any training period. Progress in learning does not always register in daily output. While learning correctness of "form" and developing the ability to reach quality standards, output may not show a daily increase and the supervisor, as well as the worker, may not be wise to measure his progress solely by it.

Then there is social approval. Any experienced supervisor knows the value of recognition as a stimulation of interest in the job.

The effectiveness of all these ways of reaching the worker's interests and relating them to the job lies in the fact that a person reacts as a whole. Sometimes we talk of training his muscles or his brain or his hands. This really isn't so. His entire self is being trained by every experience he has. The man is taught, not his hand. When he has mastered a skill, the whole man has it, uses it, and is proud of it. The person himself has ambitions to which the job may or may not be related: He either enjoys doing it, or is indifferent to it. The worker himself basks in the appreciation of his fellow workers when they recognize that he has done the job well. Anything which connects with his interest affects all parts of him. Recognition of success in one part of the job reacts to heighten his interest in the job as a whole, and he does the whole job better. Conversely, a failure in any part of the job may depress the whole person, his work and his attitude toward the job, unless through his supervisor, he comes to regard the failure as a challenge, analyzes it, and learns how to overcome it and profit from it.

The largest factor a supervisor has to deal with is his workers' interests. This emphasizes again the need for the supervisor to become well acquainted with his workers as persons, to understand their backgrounds and experience, their hopes and purposes for the future, their bents and traits and special interests and abilities, all in order that he may help them to discover and realize lasting and real connections between themselves and their jobs.

The frequent failure of management to win its deserved share of employee loyalty is often attributable to its ineptness in communications.

If it were proposed to enact a law requiring governors on automobiles so they could not go faster than 10 miles an hour, people would not stand for it. The reason is simple enough: It would affect the individual in an area where he is interested and where he has strong feelings. He has both information and motivation. But propose that a progressive income tax be imposed on corporations, which would certainly have the effect of putting a governor on the motor of our industrial machine, and he may very well remain indifferent.

This is a very serious matter, for, tenuous though the connection may seem to the average citizen, his opinions about the forces molding our civilization are, in the last analysis, controlling. If he is in favor of them, they survive. If he is opposed to them, they die. If he is indifferent to them, then that too is a form of decision, and results flow from it. The fact is that in a republic, the citizens control anything they really want to control.

If large numbers of citizens are convinced that business is evil and dangerous, it automatically follows that large numbers of legislators, senators, congressmen, members of state legislatures and city councilmen will try to derive political advantages from that emotion. Conversely, if the general public knows something about business and industry, and thinks well of them, then you can be sure that large numbers of politicians will feel the same way.

There can be little doubt that the very nature of our socio-economic environment is itself a compelling imperative for management to strive for the loyalty of its employees.

Different companies approach the accomplishment of this goal in different ways. But with most, there is a common thread which weaves its way between the approach of one company and that of another. Most companies try to win their employees' loyalty by striving to meet the objectives of employee-relations programs in the areas of wages and benefits, as well as in additional human satisfactions. Such objectives usually include: (1) good pay, (2) good working conditions, (3) good supervision, (4) opportunity for advancement, (5) steady work, (6) respectful and dignified treatment, and (7) recognition for accomplishment. These are generally viewed as the main things that really count with employees, although not necessarily always listed in the above numerical order. However, as is the case with many politicians, many companies tend to forget their platform promises during day-to-day administration. It also goes without saying that an individual supervisor's philosophy must be in harmony and in accord with that of his company. But presuming his management pursues some of the same objectives as are mentioned above, he can be the company's most effective instrument for achieving them. Such objectives place human and corporate relations programs on a par with production and marketing. Such programs essentially fashion a "way of life" in corporate relations, not only with employees, but also with the stockholders and citizens of the plant community and others. Of course, relations with each of these groups are part of a greater whole, and this whole is perhaps greater than the sum of its parts. Such a search for rewarding relationships must naturally thus be continuous and specific. The company must seek constructive and mutually rewarding relationships with all its employees, and cultivate this objective in a practical fashion. In the course of this, management behavior and communications are crucial factors. There has never been a time in American history when employees needed to know more about the problems and progress of the business which provides them a livelihood, if they are to be inspired to help their company succeed and maintain employment in the face of intensifying foreign and domestic competition. An eager and interested audience awaits management's response since employees have repeatedly expressed their desire to be kept fully informed on matters affecting the business and their job security, and also on union relations matters as well.

If it is any comfort to members of management, unions are having some rough times these days. As an official of the United Auto Workers put it, "All the things we fought for, the corporation is now giving the workers. What we have to find are other things the worker wants which the employer is not willing to give him, and we have to develop our program around these things as reasons for belonging to the union. We're searching—we're searching." This almost wistful comment underscores the basic dilemma of unions today. With the lot of the employee so much improved in the past 20 years, the unions now fear they are facing slow decline. Management has never been in a more favorable climate to engage in honorable, legal and good-faith competition for the loyalty of its employees. But it can only achieve its fair share of this by consistent good-faith behavior and utilization of all available communication media. A representative company which exemplifies this philosophy is the General Electric Co. This firm genuinely and definitely feels that the best solution to today's industrial relations problems lies in the three basic principles of their employee relations approach: (1) genuine concern for a recognition of employees' needs; (2) honest, forthright bargaining with unions, rather than meaningless haggling; and (3) full information from both parties to employees on matters significantly affecting their interests.

Here is a company that typifies the concept that the strength of any free society is based on the assumption that its people are well informed on all issues affecting them, and here is an employer willing to put its theories into practice and engage in competition for the minds and the loyalties of its employees (and with no small amount of success). Any student of the industrial relations scene is well advised to study this employer's approach to employee relations. Although it may not yet be deemed a model, it is certainly unique, innovative and thought-provoking to the student. And while one may not accord with their union-relations philosophy, their communication program must be admired.

Chrysler Corporation is another firm which recognized the value of exchanging and sharing views and opinions with its employees. In this company, the attitude emanates from the top and such is reflected in some comments by its president, Lynn A. Townsend:

> Every member of management must understand that effective communication is an essential tool of good management; and that part of his job is to relay and interpret appropriate information and news, whether good or bad, to his subordinates and superiors....
>
> There is a need to inform employees about matters which affect them or their jobs, to interpret management's position on relevant issues, to persuade employees to take actions best designed to serve the long-range mutual interests of themselves and the corporation.
>
> Most employees basically want to help a business get better — and this is very significant. But we've got to talk and listen to them. And we've got to do it regularly, not on an on-and-off basis. ... To unblock upward communication channels is to tap a great reservoir of creative opinions and suggestions which can be of great help in attaining the legitimate goals of the corporation.[132]

Communication as such is not a goal, but a means to a goal. What is sought is the development of understanding support among a team of employees, including all management people, for they, of course, are employees too. The goal is not to propagandize or to sell a "bill of goods." It is simply to achieve recognition of the individual — whatever his or her job may be — in all daily relationships. Whether you want to call it development of greater loyalty, or better morale, or company spirit, or esprit de corps, you are still headed the right way. The success of the company, and in turn the success of its employees, is greatly dependent upon teamwork of personnel at all levels. This teamwork will often be in direct ratio to the quality of the communications between each level.

Talking to the employee, and listening to him, are merely a couple of ways in which management can assure the employee that he is valued as a person. Therefore, respect for the dignity of the individual is an important communications objective also. Because it emphasizes respect for the individuality and dignity of each employee and encourages his development, enlightened management believes that the most enduring and satisfactory personnel relations will be attained by means of consultation and explanation—up and down the organization through all the channels of communication available to it.

Contrary to some misconceptions, the foreman cannot find the answers to dealing with his workers from some book. He must know his people himself. He must look to them for most of such answers. What he finds in them has been implanted in their daily experiences from childhood on. His own, as well as their, interpretive judgment is based on stimuli resulting from religious, economic, and social background. Relationships with parents, sisters, brothers and friends; their illnesses, sexual experiences and growth; their love relationships; the toughness they've acquired from collisions in the competitive world, and the shields they build to prevent it from encroaching on the soft core essential to their ideals; everything they read; every person they meet and every conversation they have; every admiration and hate they develop; every defeat and every triumph, often in trivial matters, which affect their psyche, not their worldly stance; these and infinitely more leave their marks inside each of them. Every man is a conglomerate enterprise, and his values and judgments derive from a mysterious jumble of life's acquisitions.

A supervisor's expert knowledge of a job, as an operator knows it, is not sufficient by itself to make him a good supervisor. In some cases such knowledge may even make it more difficult for him to notice, or to handle, other supervisory problems.

It shouldn't be overlooked that to a worker a job means more than a paycheck every week or the performance of certain mechanical operations over and over. To him it also means that he is a part of an organization, a needed and valuable part, wherein he has a particular and meaningful place. It means that he is a human being, a person with feelings and needs, who wonders what kinds of people his fellow workers are, what they think of him, what they expect from him, what kind of boss he has, and what he expects from him. Consequently, it is also a function of the supervisor to help the worker to adjust himself to his surroundings, to give him an idea of the organization of which he is a part, and of where he fits into it.

The supervisor faced with getting out a product, and all of those attendant difficulties, may easily overlook the problems and difficulties of his workers. It may seem natural to him to think most of results and thereby fail to spend enough time on his people. But in getting out the product of the shop, he may more often than not find the answers to most problems through talking to, and observing the conduct of, the individual employees he supervises. The more closely he listens to their comments and encourages them to talk to him, the more fully he will know each worker as a person, and the better he will supervise.

Attainment of a company's objectives requires that they be known and understood by the entire organization. This in turn requires effective communications from the top of the organization to the bottom, and from the bottom to the top, and also horizontally among the company's plants and divisions, if any. Constant effort is required by management at all levels to make sure that the objectives and the general principles guiding company actions are known, understood, and accepted, and that the avenues of communication are kept clear and easy to access. If this is done and done faithfully and correctly, it should render rich dividends in the form of positive and improved employee attitudes toward the company.

7. The Supervisor's Labor Relations Responsibilities

The foreman's responsibility for labor relations resides in four basic areas.

His first obligation is to represent management's interests in its relationships with the union and the employees. Second, he has a corresponding responsibility to represent to the company the employees' interests in their relationship with the company. This is no less compelling an obligation than the former. Third, in order to accomplish either of the above, he has an initial responsibility to comprehend the legitimate needs, wishes and attitudes of the union and the employees. And fourth, through his understanding of these legitimate needs, to then interpret them timely and accurately on behalf of the union and the employees to the company. Although the company expects the foreman to play the role of the advocate representing its interests on a partisan basis, it must also recognize that to enable him to function effectively—with the respect, trust and confidence of the union and the employees—he must be knowledgeable, willing and at liberty to represent to the company, the union's and the employees' side of things. His cannot be a one-sided bias, solely favoring the company without consideration for or recognition of merit to the union and his subordinates' viewpoints. The supervisor who functions in this manner will inevitably render himself ineffective, thus becoming totally frustrated in the accomplishment of his objectives, through the very individuals whose cooperation he must obtain in accomplishing them.

This is not to say that the supervisor's responsibilities are limited to the area of labor relations. There are many functions he performs for management, not the least of which are his responsibilities for maintenance and improvement of quality; maintaining and improving levels of productivity and output; operating to a budget or within certain other management-imposed cost limitations; and of course, his primary responsibility in the accomplishment of all of these—the people he supervises. Anything and everything he wishes to accomplish must be achieved through and by people. This aspect certainly must be viewed by even the severest or cynical critic as the most important element of his job. It becomes an increasingly important element when those people he supervises, through whom he must accomplish his given tasks, are represented by a labor organization. When that is true, and all of this presumes that management has invested in him responsibility and authority for representing its interests with union representatives, it becomes an essential, if not the most important aspect among his responsibilities. He can only meet this obligation provided management has met its obligation to fully advise him of its labor relations philosophy—its concept of management rights—and the tools and techniques for managing, supervising and maintaining order through discipline.

Represent Management's Interests

Particular and unusual demands are placed upon supervisors. In no one area does this become obviously and critically so, more than it does when he functions within the grievance machinery. In dealing with this essential area of supervisory responsibility, this section will concern itself with providing him with a basic but sufficient understanding of his role and the union's role to enable him to satisfactorily meet this responsibility.

It all turns on a fundamental presumption that the company has invested him with the commensurate authority to be able to meet this heavy responsibility. Without such authority he can never serve his employer as a "whole" management representative. Without it he can never perform to the fullest of his supervisory and managerial potential; and his company will be the loser for it as a consequence.

The primary objective of the grievance procedure is to provide a means through which employees can raise, discuss and obtain results for their complaints against management's actions. Such procedure functions best when it supplies a mechanism which allows for the timely and expeditious handling of such workers' complaints. In its operations it also coincidentally succeeds in serving three other purposes.

First, it is a procedural tool which provides the forum through which employee complaints are aired. Second, it is an educational tool in that it provides for the development of a mutual interest idea and allows for a recognition by each party of the problems that are peculiar to the other party. Third, it allows for preventive maintenance. This is the case since it keeps open the avenues of communications between the parties, and also does so by killing problems either before they arise or before they grow too large. Hand in glove with this accomplishment is the fact that the resolution of disputes between the parties builds a body of plant precedence and common law which provides the parties with direction and guidance in other disputes, thus enhancing orderliness.

For a grievance procedure to function and meet the needs of both parties, it must contain essential ingredients to make it function properly. The most important of these are listed below.

It defines a grievance. From the company's point of view, the best possible definition of a grievance under the agreement is usually a narrow one. Customarily it would therefore provide that a grievance protests "an alleged violation of a specific provision of the labor agreement as written and expressed by the parties." From the union's point of view, the broader and more general the definition and the more encompassing its scope, the better off they are.

It provides an oral discussion step. This should be viewed as the most important working step of the grievance procedure. This is the step where the majority of disputes should be resolved, if they are susceptible to resolution. Once a grievance has been reduced to written form, the parties have a growing tendency to get locked into their respective positions, assuming unyielding attitudes. Secondly, they each realize that the final resolution of the dispute, whether the grievance is ultimately sustained or denied, will almost invariably require some written communication between the parties. Of course, the union never wants to accept a complete denial of the grievance by the company and have this remain as a living record with future precedent value. In the same connection, the company is fearful that its sustaining the grievance will produce the same result. Therefore, it is always to the mutual advantage of both parties to have an oral discussion step with each bringing to that discussion a strong desire for resolution at that point.

It provides time limits for filing and provides time limits for appealing. For the grievance procedure to serve the needs of the employees, it must obligate the parties to raise grievances promptly after their occurrence and move them along expeditiously through the various steps of the procedure to a final conclusion. Stale and souring complaints produce employee unrest and deterioration of employee morale. It further produces employee discontent and lack of faith in the orderliness of the grievance procedure. Naturally, if employees are of the opinion that the grievance procedure is not an equitable way to produce resolution for their complaints, the use of economic force as a more equitable means may seem to them to be a more desirable, or even essential alternative.

It designates the participants. Again, to insure that increasing levels of authority representing each party are present in each step of the grievance procedure, participants should be spelled out. In other words, and typically, a first step would involve the employee and/or his department steward, and the department foreman; the second step might typically involve a union committeeman or chief steward with a management general foreman, superintendent or department head. Presuming it was a three-step procedure, the last step would probably involve the union's local grievance committee and/or their international representative meeting with the plant's industrial relations representative. Changing the parties who participate in each step allows for a new and fresh look to be taken of the problem with opinions less prejudiced by confrontation in the prior step. Also, as the grievance moves into the higher steps of the procedure, it brings into the picture individuals more sophisticated and knowledgeable of the interpretation and application of the labor agreement.

It defines the amount of pay to union participants. In modern labor relations, it is customary for employees' grievances to be discussed during working hours and often during paid working time. Contracts often allow union representatives a stipulated amount of time to discuss the grievance with employee grievants and conduct some investigation. But, such time limitations tend to be only sufficiently generous to allow the union representative to adequately conduct his legitimate union business without abuse of paid time.

It limits retroactive liability. Assuming that the grievance has been raised and filed by the employees or the union within the contractual time limit, the contract normally provides that under those circumstances, the employee will be made whole if his grievance is sustained. However, while this is true, contracts usually place some time limitations on the amount of retroactive adjustment which will be provided. Therefore, if the employee files the grievance beyond the contractual time limit and such filing beyond the time limit is not construed to render his claim invalid by its untimeliness, the retroactive liability limitations in such case will not make him whole—but probably would go back only as far as to the time of his initial filing of the claim.

It gives settlement authority to the participants. Naturally, the whole exercise is meaningless if the contract does not allow the respective parties to assume sufficient authority to resolve their differences. It is equally as empty an exercise if the parties do not accept and exercise this authority when it is endowed by the contract and by their respective organizations.

It moves unresolved cases to arbitration. Even reasonable people can disagree. The parties will not always be able to resolve each dispute which arises between them. It is true that the overwhelming majority should be susceptible to resolution during the steps of the grievance procedure. But, it is also true that not all will be. For this reason, a good procedure provides that such unresolved cases will be moved—again promptly, within reasonable time limitations, to the arbitration process where they can be peacefully and equitably decided.

What is "a grievance"? Is it any dispute between the parties? Is it any complaint or problem raised by an employee? The definition of a grievance as found in the thousands of labor agreements has numerous variations. Typical of a broad and loosely worded provision is the following:

> Any dispute, disagreement or difference arising between any employee or the union and the company may be presented as a grievance.

Such a clause is generally sought by the labor union since few unions regard the contractual definition, irrespective of its verbiage, as a prohibition or limitation to the union's legitimate presentation of any employee complaint. Typically, shop stewards' manuals instruct the steward to obtain the answers to two questions in making his judgment as to whether an employee has a bona fide grievance. These typical questions are (1) has the contract been violated, or (2) has the company treated the employee unfairly?

In the union's view, if the employee's complaint can fall within the purview of either of these conditions, it is a matter which should be processed as a grievance.

As representatives of a political institution, most shop stewards feel a compulsion to press any claim made by a member employee. As adversary representatives of their special interest group, they also feel an obligation to obtain every possible extension and expansion of the benefits and privileges already provided under the labor agreement. Granted, only cases which meet the criteria of the first question above will cutomarily be processed into arbitration if unresolved. But those disputes which fall under the second question also will often be pursued by the union on behalf of the employee. And once filed, such cases must be discussed and reviewed between the parties just as fully and thoroughly as a bona fide complaint dealing with a contract violation.

Modern and experienced industrial relations professionals have come to agree that it is in the best interest of the company to have a more narrow and restrictive grievance definition. Therefore, unless the union's grievance can meet the test of involving the interpretation, application, or meaning of a particular contractual provision, it should not be considered a valid grievance. Basically, this approach is taken to prevent union attempts to further encroach on the managerial function. It is also done to resist union efforts to obtain through the channels of the grievance machinery, that which they failed to attempt, or failed to obtain at the bargaining table.

This view embraces the concept that the labor agreement represents a compromise arrived at between the parties. It springs from the management theory that the labor agreement is the only expression of those rights, privileges and benefits to which the union and the employees are entitled as a matter of contractual relationship—and any additional conditions and benefits to be enjoyed by the union and employees must be achieved only through the formal process of collective bargaining—and not otherwise achieved within the grievance machinery during the life of the contract.

Obviously such a narrow grievance definition should not be employed by the foreman as a shield to prevent him from exploring and resolving employee "complaints" which are not "grievances" as defined in the contract. The foreman must still view each employee problem with an understanding of the principles of employee and human relations and thereby treat each instance of worker discontent as a serious matter. Although a trivial matter such as a complaint over the malfunction of a coin-operated vending machine, and other like problems, may not constitute "a grievance," for the sake of continuing good employee relations, the foreman should nevertheless treat such complaints as significant and bring about some prompt solution.

What is not a grievance? Presuming that the labor agreement does not provide otherwise, the following matters are typical of those usually deemed to be within the exclusive province of management, and, therefore, not appropriate subject for a valid grievance:

- Location of plants
- Selection and hiring of work force
- Size of work force
- Selection and control of supervisors
- Establishment and elimination of jobs
- Internal organization of plant
- Type of product to be manufactured
- Control of the methods of operation
- Control of the quality requirements
- Price establishment
- Sales practices and advertising
- Control and protection of plant properties

Management generally adheres strongly to the proposition that residual powers rest with the company. Therefore, the foreman should always assume the position that he does not need to look into the collective bargaining agreement to determine what rights management has reserved to itself—but should look to the agreement only to establish what rights it has ceded away to the employees and union. The best method for getting the union into the idea of assuming their burden of establishing their case is to insist upon their answering two questions relative to any grievance which is processed: what provision is alleged violated, and how did the company violate this provision.

Requiring them to do so has several distinct advantages:

• It tends to contain the argument within the terms and provisions of the labor agreement.

• It keeps the discussion or meeting more disciplined and businesslike.

• If the union is unable to produce sound argument as to "what" or "how," it may serve as a discouragement with regard to further appeals. It may reveal to the union the weakness and shortcomings of their case and cause them to think twice about processing it further.

• In arbitration, it enables the company to point out inconsistencies, if any, in union arguments. When arguing "what provision is allegedly violated" the union may first select a given contract clause in support of their contentions only to abandon it later in favor of another when the first takes them down a fruitless path. In changing their argument, it is very possible for them to be inconsistent or contradictory in their positions, when one is compared against the other. The same may also result from their changing positions on "How did the company violate this provision." Such incompatible or incongruous positions may sometimes prove to have been damaging to their case when the matter is fully explored before an arbitrator.

The word "management" while often thought of in an impersonal way is actually a very personal designation. It should not denote or conjure up the image of plaster and bricks and mortar — it consists of people: all of those individual employees who have some degree of managerial responsibility at various levels for running the business. These people, working together as a team, and coordinating their numerous and various efforts, make up the "management."

In today's industrial organization, the foreman is a member of that management. He is, or should be, the manager of the operations placed under his responsibility. In this capacity, he should function in the first step of the grievance procedure and be invested with the authority of management in his handling, answering and denying or sustaining grievances. The employees under the foreman's supervision look to him as a member of management. In a very large measure their view of the company will be personified by their opinion of their immediate supervisor. No matter how well the negotiators have done their job in designing and constructing the labor agreement, it will not serve the needs of the parties unless it is made to work from day to day.

The foreman's primary responsibility in labor relations matters is to administer the labor agreement with a minimum of friction but at the same time avoid any impairment of those fundamental responsibilities and rights of the company to manage the business efficiently and successfully.

The contract provisions are intended to protect the rights of the company, the employees, and the union as the collective bargaining agent of the employees. The agreement is not intended to be a one-sided document, giving advantage to management, the employees or the union. Such an idea of advantage to one party or another is foreign to the agreement — and should not be sought by the foreman in studying or applying its several provisions. The contract is intended to provide mutual benefits and protection to the company and its employees.

As a supervisor, he therefore has a personal and key responsibility to do his part to help achieve the objectives of the agreement. His role in the day-to-day administration of the agreement is a vital one. The extent to which the contract is successful in maintaining harmonious relations between the company, its employees and the union depends upon the success which the supervisor and other members of the management organization have in applying its terms justly, honestly and intelligently. A thorough understanding by the supervisor and other members of the management organization of both what he should do, and what he should avoid doing, is essential. He cannot carry out his responsibilities and do a good labor relations job if he is poorly informed regarding the manner in which he should function within the grievance machinery. Having the proper knowledge and skill in these matters will provide him with the confidence and the tools necessary to accomplish a good job in this important area of his responsibility.

Again, the supervisor is urged to remember that the labor agreement does not necessarily incorporate all of the terms and conditions satisfactory or favorable to management, the union and the employees. It is a compromise of the needs of management, the union and the employees. His job as a foreman is not to be a "judge" of what is fair or unfair, but to perform his role by operating in good faith in accordance with the terms and provisions of the agreement, preserving and protecting those management rights which remain, and seeing to it that the employees receive the specific benefits to which they are entitled under the agreement. A concurrent obligation inherent in his job is to insure that the obligations of the company to the employees and the union under the agreement are fulfilled.

Represent Employees' Interests

Do not assume the posture that supervisors represent management, and the union represents the workers. You're only doing half your whole job if you do—and you're letting the union do the best half. Employees will turn to their union stewards and representatives when they come to the conclusion that going to their supervisor is an exercise in frustration or futility. Many come to this conclusion. Employees have problems. Employees are not always in the wrong; management is not always in the right. Employees have needs, interests, goals and opinions. If they take the time to find out, some supervisors will learn that their workers are not so much different from themselves. That could be a disturbing discovery for some.

Being an employee, especially an employee of a large organization, necessarily leads to the loss of a great deal of independence. Instead of making his own decisions, an employee (whether he is a manager or a worker) responds to the decisions of other people. Instead of acting independently to control his own life and career, an employee gives up this control and becomes dependent upon his superiors and his organization. This loss of control is especially noticeable for decisions related to his own career. Instead of acting for his own interests, an employee is expected to work for the good of his organization and leave decisions which affect him to other people.

Some conflict between the individual's needs and desires and the demands of the organization is inevitable, regardless of the level the individual occupies in the organization. Some of the more important conflicts are between the organization's need for control and predictability and the individual's desire for freedom and independence; between the organization's need for standardization and the individual's desire for variety and enjoyable work; between the organization's demand for loyalty (even unquestioning loyalty) and the individual's belief that his primary loyalties should be to himself, his ideals, his future, and his family.

How can a supervisor determine for himself if he is doing what he can in representing his workers with the company they both share employment in?

In the following pages I've provided a framework of questions which a supervisor may ask himself regarding his organization, his workers, their operations, and about himself. It should go without saying. for any beneficial results to ever come from such a review, introspective, soul-searching, sincere and wholly honest answers must be supplied. You're only kidding yourself otherwise. Employees know what the truthful answers would be.

• Do you afford an opportunity for your workers to advance before hiring new employees to fill a vacant job?

• Do you represent your workers to higher management? Do you speak up for them—take up for them when they're right—and argue with your superiors about decisions which you consider wrong, which will negatively affect your people?

- Do you feel responsible for them while they are at work?
- Do you concern yourself with their problems away from work?
- Do your workers need a spokesman on their behalf, or do they already have one in you?
- Do you keep your office door open, so to speak, or is this a myth for public consumption only?
- Do you show an interest in your workers by keeping them informed on all matters which may affect them?
- Do you see that your employees get everything that's coming to them — full wages, benefits, contractual conditions — and protest on their behalf if they are not?
- Do you complain to management about wage or hour or working conditions inequities?
- Do you give workers a chance to improve their skills, or otherwise prepare them for better jobs?
- Do you follow up on educational programs so that employees' newly acquired knowledge can be put to use?
- Do you see to it that they have adequate lighting, heat and ventilation?
- Do you see to it that their lunch, toilet and clean-up facilities are kept clean and orderly?
- Do you see to it that the machines, tools, and equipment you oversee are kept in good working order and in a safe and healthful condition?
- Do you nurture and maintain a close relationship between you and those you supervise?
- Do you act promptly and effectively to correct problems as they arise?
- Do you treat all workers fairly, consistently and without favoritism?
- Do you follow up on promises you make to them?
- Do you solicit and utilize their ideas, opinions, suggestions and constructive criticisms?
- Do you follow up on decisions based on complaints to ascertain (1) the remedy has been applied, (2) the problem has been resolved, and (3) what the affect is on morale?
- Do you work on your ability to teach and to communicate with your people?
- Do you have communications regularly with your people to know what they're thinking, how they're doing, what problems they're experiencing?

• Do you treat your people as humans — ones who hear, see, talk, and feel — or as workers, who are only there to work?

Your employees will ultimately know whether you have answered these questions in good faith, and whether you have, or have not, acted responsively to produce desirable changes where needed.

Comprehend Employee Needs

In order to accomplish and satisfy the prior responsibilities, the supervisor has an initial responsibility to comprehend the legitimate needs, wishes and attitudes of the union and the employees.

As of 1981, some 83 million Americans are holding full- or part-time jobs. Of the total — 62 percent of them men — about 19 million are engaged in manufacturing and one million of these are tied to the dull, routine tedium of an assembly line like that satirized four decades ago by Charlie Chaplin in *Modern Times*. But there are actually more white-collar workers (49 percent of the total) than blue (35 percent); the rest are service workers and farm workers. There are more women at work in the nation today than ever before, and more young people.

The mood of this vast work force is obviously of tremendous importance to the country, as a whole as well as to the individuals themselves. Worker attitudes affect productivity — how competitive the nation is versus nations such as Japan and how high America's standard of living can go. On a more philosophical, but no less significant level, a nation's attitude toward work is a reflection of its sense of itself. The work ethic involves not only a job but a way of life.

While people have been complaining about work since it was invented, there is a widespread feeling that there is something different about today's discontent. As a result, the managers of American business and industry are now coming up with plan after plan — some pure public relations, some quite innovative. Literally hundreds of companies have instituted "job enrichment" programs to give workers a sense of satisfaction on the job and send them home with a feeling of accomplishment.

In the automobile industry, where about 25 percent of the work force assembles cars with robotlike monotony, General Motors experimented with a "team" approach to the assembly of its new $130,000 motor home. Rather than having the chassis roll down an assembly line, with each worker performing only one or two functions, teams ranging in size from three to six workers are now building selected coaches from hubcap to horn. Ford has tried a team assembly program at its Saline, Michigan, parts plant while Chrysler has given some Detroit area plants virtual carte blanche to try any experiment they choose. So far, these have ranged from employees operating without a foreman to assigning assembly-line workers the relatively pleasant chore of test-driving the new cars they have just built.

While such experiments by the auto industry's Big Three are still inconclusive, others are not. Indiana Bell Telephone, for example, used to assemble its telephone books in 21 steps, each performed by a different clerk. It now gives each clerk individual responsibility for assembling an entire book. One result: employee turnover in recent years has been cut by as much as 50 percent.

There is ample reason to believe that experiments will continue and new solutions to the problems of undesirable work will continue to be sought. Though the problems of the workplace have a long history, they are being rediscovered by a new and less patient generation. Lousy jobs are not illusions created by the work reformers. The interest these experiments have generated will surely stimulate greater awareness and stir new demands for improved work.

Today, a wide range of employee-motivation experiments like these are being tried across the country. Employers are realizing that people are capable of doing far more than their jobs either require or allow, that if they actually enjoy their work they will perform better. Work must not be simply the penalty that a man pays to survive; it must be something that offers meaning in and of itself. Structuring jobs to be more meaningful and satisfying not only fulfills a social responsibility to those employed, but it is good business as well.

The many sources of job dissatisfaction are conditions under the very noses of the managing and directing supervisors. Claiming ignorance of the reasons for worker unrest or discontent is not a viable excuse. It is part of a supervisor's job to realize and comprehend the problems, needs, wishes and attitudes of his workers.

With a supervisor's help and concern, many of these conditions creating worker dissatisfaction can be diminished and controlled. Man is an animal with a conscience. Not only will he accept responsibility, he wants it. Many even thrive upon it. Every person is creative — *every person*. And which side do you want the creativity on? If it's not working for you, it may very well be working against you. With a supervisor's interest, attention and assistance, he can help to reduce employee discontent and participate in a turnaround of employee attitudes and cooperation. But first he must analyze them and correctly determine their causes and the alternative and necessary cures.

Interpret the Union and the Employees to the Company

The unions' traditional philosophy has been, if you want to enrich jobs, enrich the paycheck. The better the wage, the better the job satisfaction.

Not necessarily, according to job-enrichment advocates, and evidently, even workers themselves. When University of Michigan researchers asked 1,533 workers at all occupational levels to rank 25 aspects of work in order of importance, "interesting work" ranked first. Second was "enough help and equipment to get the job done," followed by "enough information to get the job done" and "enough authority to get the job done." Placing next: "good pay." After that came "opportunity to develop special abilities," "job security," and "seeing the results of one's work."

Work has to be organized in such a way as to help people derive self-satisfaction in performing it.

The problem is of course a basic one: Those things that are in the enlightened self-interest of society as a whole, are not necessarily in the competitive self-interest of all companies.

Perhaps there is little that one supervisor alone can do to change the structure of things established by organization authority high above him. However, he is well-positioned to hear and see and know what the workers are saying, feeling, thinking and wanting.

It is always interesting to witness the traditional experience of union officials sitting across the table from management during collective bargaining and telling the company what its own workers want, and why certain things are on their minds — often to the surprise, even the dismay of management. Where does management get its information about employees' wishes, attitudes and expectations? Of course from employees — but also, from plant union stewards and representatives. From people no closer to the workers than the company's supervisors themselves.

If supervisors are doing their "whole" job, there are few reasons why, at any given point in time, they cannot interpret fairly accurately and fully, what the company's workers are thinking.

Of course, it should go without saying, such information will only be as beneficial as the good uses management makes of it.

A supervisor's primary responsibility is the handling of other human beings. Nothing has greater importance, nor should anything be given a higher ranking. A man's complexity as a human being presents the challenge and the opportunity for you to bring out the best in him, and the best in you.

The largest factor with which a supervisor has to deal is his workers' interests. This emphasizes again the need for the supervisor to become well acquainted with his people as persons, to understand their backgrounds and experience, their hopes and purposes for the future, their bents and traits and special interests and abilities, so that he may help them to discover and realize lasting connections between themselves and their jobs.

8. Arbitral Arenas

Duty of Fair Representation

The majority of today's labor agreements contain elaborate provisions for union security, with the most prevalent clause being a "union shop" arrangement. Under such a clause, all employees must obtain and maintain membership in the union as a condition of continued employment. Presuming the agreement contains instead a type of union security clause allowing employees the option of joining or refraining from joining the union, some employees may choose the latter. However, irrespective of the union's preference in such a case, *it has an obligation to represent all employees* in the bargaining unit for the purpose of collective bargaining over wages, hours, and other terms and conditions of employment — whether the employees are members of the union or not. Despite such a legal requirement, typically the union may give discriminatory representation, particularly regarding those employees who are hardcore holdouts.

The courts have held that unions must be accorded broad discretion in handling individual grievances. But they are not entitled to absolute immunity. They do owe a duty of fair representation. And a union can become liable in damages for breaching this duty.

The duties owed by unions to employees in handling grievances are more fully examined by Houselowe in "Individual Rights in Collective Labor Relations."[133] It is arguable that, whatever the needs for flexibility and wide discretion in the negotiation of new or the modification of existing collective contracts, no such flexibility is either needed or appropriate when rights under a contract are involved. The standards for judgment in this area have been less than perfectly formulated. In general terms they are frequently stated as follows: The union's conduct must not be willful, arbitrary, capricious, or discriminatory. The union must not have declined to press the grievance out of laziness or prejudice, or out of unwillingness to expend money on behalf of nonmembers. Its decisions with respect to individual grievances must have been honest and reasonable.

The rejection of a grievance by the union must have been on the merits, in the exercise of honest discretion and/or sound judgment, following a complete and fair investigation. The rejection must not have been because of bad faith or fraud. The bargaining agent must not have acted in a negligent manner.

In any event, the foreman's approach to the handling and resolution of grievances involving nonmember employees whose claims may be mishandled by the union should be no different than that accorded the member employee. He must still use the labor agreement as the only basis for judging the issue and applying any remedy.

In handling the grievances of nonmembers, the supervisor should be aware of two particular provisions of the Labor Management Relations Act with regard to the rights of employees. In section 7 of the act:

> Employees shall have the right to self-organization, to form, join, or assist labor organizations, to bargain collectively through representatives of their own choosing, and to engage in other concerted activities for the purpose of collective bargaining or other mutual aid or protection, and shall also have the right to refrain from any or all of such activities except to the extent that such right may be affected by an agreement requiring membership in a labor organization as a condition of employment as authorized in section 8(s)(3).

The second provision of the act that comes into play most often under this type of union security clause is section 9(a):

> Representatives, designated or selected for the purposes of collective bargaining by the majority of the employees in a unit appropriate for such purposes, shall be the exclusive representatives for all employees in such unit for the purposes of collective bargaining in respect to rates of pay, wages, hours of employment, or other conditions of employment: provided, that any individual employee or a group of employees shall have the right at any time to present grievances to their employer and to have such grievances adjusted, without the intervention of the bargaining representative, as long as the adjustment is not inconsistent with the terms of a collective bargaining contract or agreement then in effect: provided further, that the bargaining representative has been given opportunity to be present at such adjustment.

The grievance process must be afforded to nonmembers as well as union members and on the same terms and conditions. Any grievance should be viewed in the light of the basic standards established by the terms of the contract between the company and the union. All grievances, including those from nonmembers, must be limited to problems within the scope of this standard. Any relief or remedy applied must not violate or undermine this basic standard.

Under the management right clause, the company has retained the right to manage and direct the working forces. In so doing, its representatives must necessarily converse and discuss with employees, issue them instructions and orders, ask them questions, give them information. It may not "bargain" with them individually regarding their wages, hours, working conditions, and so on. It may not endeavor to enter into individual "agreements" with them covering such subjects.

The duty of fair representation has been interpreted in various ways by the courts, and these interpretations indicate that the problems involved are as numerous as the possible solutions to these problems. The problems arise generally as a result of vagaries in the law and in collective bargaining agreements, but labor experts are at odds as to how to remedy the problems.

The duty of fair representation can be traced to its origin in the Railway Labor Act and the landmark decision of *Vaca v. Sipes* (US SUPCT, 1967, LRRM 2369) which established the standard of "arbitrariness" to determine whether a union has breached its duty to its members. But the use of the standard is a "traumatic experience" because it is difficult to apply in a legal context. An equitable accommodation of rights is needed to strike the balance between the employee's right to press his grievance, the union's contractual obligations to the employer and its statutory obligations to the employee, and the employer's sometimes conflicting obligations to bother the employee and the union.

In fair representation cases, employees have the option to pursue the employer and the union through the contract and through the courts. Because of this grant to individuals of a variety of methods to pursue victims to proceed against, corrective action in this area is long overdue.

In judicial proceedings, juries have "usurped the arbitrator's role." Unions have been held liable for breach of the duty of fair representation without a showing of breach of the contract and without any arbitration award against the employer. What is needed is an "allocation statement" by the Supreme Court on the burden of proof of the parties' competing interests.

The problems involved in fair representation cases could be alleviated to a degree by "lawyer-free" enforcement of the bargaining agreement. Swift and nonlegal contract administration would be superior to the current protracted arbitration and litigation proceedings.

Varying Standards

Since the Supreme Court's holding in *Vaca v. Sipes*, decisions in fair representation cases have been getting "screwier and screwier." There are varying standards for determining breach of this duty, including "negligence," "arbitrary and capricious," "bad faith," and "invidious," all used by the courts in what amounts to a case-by-case determination.

Although the Supreme Court has determined that Joint Area Committees (JACs) within the Teamster's jurisdiction are arbitration boards, the JACs must be "circumscribed" to protect the rights of the individual employees in arbitration proceedings. With regard to any legislative proposals to define the parameters of the duty of fair representation, eventually such a proposal would end up as an amendment to the Taft-Hartley Act. The "cleansing effect" of the duty of fair representation on unions and employers still exists, and a "decent job" of meeting that duty by unions and employers is going to the ultimate benefit of employees.

Problems have arisen in this area due to "conceptual difficulties" of the law. *Vaca v. Sipes* made a distinction between the union's breach as a tort and the employee's right to press his grievance under the bargaining agreement. Recent decisions indicate that a union may be held liable for breaching its duty to an employee, even though the employee was discharged for cause within the meaning of the bargaining agreement, if the union fails to fully address the employee's grievance.

Although an employee may pursue his grievance in arbitration or in court, in fact the issue is one of remedies, not forums. In an arbitration proceeding under the agreement, an arbitration is limited to "make whole" remedies, whereas in court an employee may be awarded traditional remedies including damages. An amendment to the Taft-Hartley would result from efforts to define this area of law, but a finding of breach of the bargaining agreement should be based only on determination that the breach "seriously undermines the arbitral process."

Developments in Arbitration

Expediting the Arbitration Process. In limited situations, particularly where there is a large accumulation of grievances, the parties may wish to expedite arbitration procedures to their mutual satisfaction and benefit.

For example, an expedited procedure was adopted by one union and employer to cut the costs and time involved in arbitrating a backlog of grievances. Under the expedited procedure, (1) each party prepares a written statement of the grievance and facts and submits a copy to the other party; (2) each party states its thinking as to how the facts fit the contract, again with a copy to the other party; (3) both parties seek to arrive at a joint statement, but failing that, their diverse views are submitted to the arbitrator; and (4) the arbitrator holds a hearing where he asks questions and listens to statements limited to facts and opinions submitted in the aforementioned statements. No posthearing briefs are filed and no opinion accompanies the award unless the arbitrator feels that comments are needed (an award without an opinion would not serve as a precedent under their plan but could be used "as a basis for conversation").

The following possibilities for expediting arbitration proceedings should be considered:

1. Dry run arbitration;
2. Prehearing statements;
3. Avoidance of "brinkmanship" prior to actual arbitration;
4. Greater use of submission agreements;
5. More effective use of factual stipulations and consequent reduced use of witnesses;
6. Elimination of transcripts, except under special circumstances;
7. Elimination of posthearing briefs;
8. Drastic shortening of opinions;
9. Early issuance of award with brief statement of reasoning, followed later by full opinion;
10. Greater use of memorandum opinions or even the equivalent of bench rulings;
11. Increased use of "instant" arbitration;
12. Expanded use of the hearing officer technique for routine cases under guidance of senior arbitrators.

One or more of the above possibilities may have real utility in a particular case. Judgment obviously must be exercised by the parties and their arbitrator in determining which, if any, of the possibilities are desirable and of beneficial promise for the given parties or for the given case.

Examples of Expedited Procedures. Limited time-strictures on the arbitrator are unusual, but many industries are "expediting" their arbitration procedures.

Steel. The procedure devised by the United Steelworkers and U.S. Steel is an example. Here members of special panels of arbitrators — and not the umpire — hear the so-called "one-shot" grievances. The decisions are short, and, the parties agree, cannot be used as precedent.

Brewery. A novel system was developed by the Teamsters and Anheuser Busch Brewery Company. Formerly unresolved grievances were submitted to a multiplant grievance committee consisting of company and union appointees. But this committee often deadlocked, and the time required to process grievances to arbitration was unsatisfactory. The union and its members demanded a more responsive approach.

Following a four-month strike over contractual issues, the parties redesigned the grievance and arbitration procedure so that no dispute would take more than two months to resolve. They placed a permanent neutral on the multiplant grievance committee (which now became a five-member body), and they arranged for monthly meetings of this committee so that there would be no delay at the final stage.

The new approach operated in this way:

1. The committee "rides the circuit," meeting in a different city each month.

2. Before a case is appealed to the committee, the local parties stipulate all the facts, both those agreed-on and in disupte; and they secure affidavits to support their respective versions of the disputed facts.

3. They then present their fact stipulations, affidavits, and arguments to the committee. Witnesses are rarely present.

4. The committee goes into executive session. If the company and union members disagree on the disposition, the neutral casts the deciding vote and prepares a brief opinion to explain it.

In this manner, 20 to 30 cases are disposed of in two or three days.

The neutral member finds himself playing many roles. He is an arbitrator when his vote resolves the deadlock, but in other cases he may serve as a consultant, mediator, or sounding board.

One of the reasons for the frequent meetings and immediate decisions is the "status quo" provision in the agreement. Management cannot carry out most disciplinary actions and some subcontracting, if protested, unless the committee has heard the disputes and resolved it in management's favor.

This system contains a built-in danger: When the arbitration forum becomes so accessible and the process so speedy, the local parties may not bother to try to settle their differences. It is easier to let the committee provide a quick answer. A new creative effort may therefore by required to prevent the erosion of responsibility at the local level.

Fabricating. A unique procedure is used by Allis Chalmers and the Machinists Union at some Pennsylvania plants. The parties obtain dates from the arbitrator. When a date is agreed upon, they send him written briefs which he studies on the specified date and then renders a short decision without opinion. He may, however, ask for a hearing. This procedure is used only where there is no dispute about the facts.

Airlines. Some employers and unions in the airline industry have also traveled the expedited route. This industry is characterized by tripartite system boards of adjustment. It is also known for unique grievances. Let me share one such with you.

An airline passenger agent at St. Louis, with time on his hands, decided to perfect his skills on the computer keyboard at the ticket counter. He typed out: "Now is the time for all good men to go f_____ themselves." As he typed, the words appeared on that little green computer screen above the keyboard. Then along came a buddy who looked at the screen, leaned over, and pushed the button marked "Enter." By this action he conveyed the message to the computer. Seconds later, in a printout at company headquarters, there appeared this most unusual directive from St. Louis. The passenger agent was disciplined. An arbitration ensued.

Well, the arbitrator listened with a straight face. He heard a witness explain that words and phrases can be removed from the computer's memory only by using predetermined symbols, but there is no known key for the passsenger agent's magic phrase. Thus, at any time, at any station or ticket office, someone may accidentally cue the computer in, and there will appear on a small green screen, "Now is the time for all good men to . . ."

It should also be known that arbitrators occasionally turn the tables. One such instance occurred during a hearing concerned with the propriety of a rule banning male flight attendants from wearing beards. The arbitrator, as fortune would have it, was one of our attractive nonmale colleagues. As part of its case, the union brought in a dozen or so neatly bearded, currently employed airline employees from various classifications to show how unreasonable the rule was. After the men, one more handsome than the man who had preceded him, had been paraded before the arbitrator, she announced demurely: "I'm not sure whether these gentlemen are witnesses or exhibits. But you should know, if they are the latter, that it has always been my practice to take exhibits home to study at my leisure!"

But, back to "expedition." Eastern Air Lines and the Machinists Union have created what they call a "time controlled" procedure. There are no transcripts or written briefs. Each side has one hour in which to present its case and must include, within the hour, its opening and closing arguments, direct examination of its own witnesses, and cross-examination of the opposing party's witnesses.

Broadcasting. In what must be one of the earliest expedited procedures, the National Association of Broadcast Engineers and Technicians and the National Broadcasting Company agreed, in 1959, that the parties could request arbitration of certain disputes within 48 hours of an occurrence, and the arbitrator was to hear the case within 72 hours thereafter and to render an award within 48 hours after the close of the hearing.

The procedure worked well, but grievances began to accumulate at an unusual rate. The umpire then suggested what came to be called "mediation." Under this procedure, the parties selected a series of grievances, summarized the facts and their positions on each case, and presented the material to the umpire, who attempted to settle them through mediation. If mediation failed, he decided the issues immediately, based on the information contained in the written statements and arguments.

A new provision in the 1985 agreement permitted either party to file a grievance directly with the umpire, who had to commence his hearings not more than 24 hours later. The umpire had to render his award no later than 24 hours after the close of the hearing, but he could send his opinion later. In this unusual industry, where time is of the essence and the show must go on, the umpire was given authority to provide injunctive or any other appropriate relief.

It became apparent to the umpire, after a while, that considerable time was spent at the hearings in discussions which would normally take place at the first step of the grievance procedure. At his suggestion, a preliminary step was established to provide for an ad hoc exchange between the parties before they appeared at the arbitration hearing.

By 1986, the office of the umpire was flooded with requests for expedited arbitrations, and NBC and NABET sought to stem the tide. In their 1986 Master Agreement they established a combination of local umpires and a national umpire, and they confined the expedited procedure to complaints concerning actions not yet effectuated. It was utilized only when time did not permit the processing of a grievance in the regular procedure. But the parties also underscored their intention to permit changes in operations to take effect pending the outcome of an arbitration.

In the first year of its operation, the system reportedly worked fairly well, reducing the number of grievances submitted under the expedited procedure and heard by the national umpire, and permitting more availability for the "emergency" cases. The preliminary interchange also helped to reduce the number of disputes submitted for arbitration.

Federal Grievance Arbitration

The Congress stumbled badly in its efforts to provide the federal sector with the first statutory grievance arbitration system in history.

The congressional purpose in writing this section of the 1978 Civil Service Reform Act was to produce a reasonably accurate facsimile of the private sector grievance system complete with final and binding arbitration. However, Congress produced a somewhat different animal. Among other problems, the resultant system is anything but final and binding in its effects.

The practical effect of the badly designed procedure will be widespread confusion, many lengthy delays, and the likely impairment, rather than improvement, of management-employee relations according to many arbitrators. It is readily apparent that arbitration in the federal sector is intended to reflect the traditional model of arbitration as practiced for many years in the unionized side of private business and industry. However, congressional drafters wound up rather wide of the mark. Instead of a relatively simple arbitration system for helping to reduce employer-employee tensions, Congress dished up a labyrinth that almost appears to mock law as a tool of governance.

Instead of focusing on the final aspects of arbitration as the cornerstone of the policy, Congress treated arbitration as a mere prelude to an elaborate panoply of appeals and advisory mechanisms. The very nature of grievance arbitration is changed and its effectiveness is diminished by such an approach. As a sample of the problem, there are eight different points in the statutory plan for arbitrating grievances involving discrimination where the aggrieved employee has an opportunity to move the matter to the federal court.

By contrast with the private sector scheme where the appealing of arbitral decisions is a rarity and where such appeals often involve limited judicial review, the 1978 law provides extensive appeal procedures. In some of these, the courts are directed to conduct brand-new trials on the issues in the case.

Also deplored is the congressional failure to banish the General Accounting Office from the federal arbitration scene. Under the pre–1978 Executive Order on grievances in the federal service, the GAO had been widely criticized for playing "a bull-in-the-china shop" role in the arbitration process. Despite a 1978 congressional effort to indicate that such interference must cease, GAO's incursions into the handling of those cases have persisted. A revised statute should "finally and fully eliminate the GAO from a role in these proceedings."

If fraud is alleged, already existing criminal processes should be used. The GAO has "grudgingly" recognized that the 1978 law authorized arbitrators to order back pay to remedy improper discharges and other disciplines. But meanwhile, the GAO continues to intervene in other ways in these cases. By the continued demonstration of its historic antipathy to arbitration and by its tradition of interference, the GAO " will continue to thwart" the policy goals of reducing employee-employer tensions. It appears that the only surcease for the federal system will be a flat and full congressional ban on such interventions.

Congress will have a very difficult and delicate task "to untie the complications" of the arbitration sections of the 1978 law. Nevertheless, it is possible to amend the statute to produce a process that is more of "the traditional model of (private) arbitration" than the present law. This traditional process has been successful in "resolving commercial disputes for the last four centuries, and labor disputes for at least the last two generations."[134]

The basic function of the grievance procedure and arbitration in private employment is to assure compliance with the collective bargaining agreement. While this is also a key function of the grievance procedure and arbitration in the federal sector, another is to review or police compliance with controlling laws, rules, and regulations by federal agency employers and employees alike.

The dual role of the grievance procedure and arbitration probably was a principal factor in the congressional decision (1) to specify that each collective agreement in the federal sector "shall" provide a grievance procedure with arbitration, (2) to specify that all grievances "shall" be subject to the grievance and arbitration procedures except those specifically excluded by the collective agreement of statute, and (3) to define the term "grievance" very broadly.

Arbitral disposition of federal-sector grievances will often be governed or materially affected by laws, rules, and regulations apart from the collective agreement; another highly significant factor is that important areas of unilateral management control in the federal sector exist by statute. For some matters in the federal sector, the collective agreement and custom cannot be made the controlling "law of the plant."

Turning now to the detailed language of the statutes, it is noted first that it is required by statute that each collective bargaining agreement in the federal sector "shall provide procedures for the settlement of grievances, including questions of arbitrability." The statute also requires that each agreement "shall ... provide that any grievance not satisfactorily settled under the negotiated grievance procedure shall be subject to binding arbitration which may be invoked by either" the union or the federal agency employer.

The same statute provides, with only two exceptions, that the contractual grievance procedure and arbitration (since the grievance procedure must provide for arbitration) "shall be the exclusive procedures for resolving grievances which fall within its coverage." The two exceptions involve certain subjects or issues for which employees are given the option of using either (but not both) the contractual grievance and arbitration procedures or certain purely statutory procedures.

The rule governing "coverage" of the contractual grievance procedure is simple. All grievances are automatically covered by the grievance procedure and can go to arbitration unless excluded by agreement of the parties or unless specifically excluded by statute. Regarding exclusions the statute provided in substance for the following:

1. Any collective bargaining agreement may exclude any matter from the application of the agreement's grievance procedure.

2. Grievances concerning the following subjects or issues specifically excluded from the grievance procedure and arbitration: (1) political activities; (2) retirement, life insurance, or health insurance; (3) suspension or removal for national security; (4) examination, certification, or appointment; (5) classification of any position if the classification does not result in the reduction in grade or pay of an employee.

What can qualify as a "grievance" in federal employment? The term "grievance" is defined very broadly as any complaint —

1. by any employee concerning any matter relating to the employment of the employee;

2. by any labor organization concerning any matter relating to the employment of any employee; or

3. by any employee, labor organization, or agency concerning the effect or interpretation, or a claim of breach, of a collective bargaining agreement; or any claimed violation, misinterpretation, or misapplication of any law, rule, or regulation affecting conditions of employment.

Thus, to reiterate, it is clear (1) that every collective agreement in the federal sector must provide a grievance procedure and arbitration, (2) that the door to the grievance procedure and arbitration is open wide to all grievances except those specifically excluded by the agreement or statute, and (3) that the term "grievance" is defined broadly with the result that an extremely wide variety of complaints will qualify for access to the grievance procedure and arbitration.

Interest Arbitration

Interest arbitration is the procedure whereby an arbitrator fills out the terms of the settlement on all the issues that the parties could not resolve themselves. The arbitrator takes on the issues on which the parties reached an impasse, and offers his binding version of how they would have resolved those issues. This kind of arbitration is to be distinguished from grievance arbitration where the award is limited much more sharply in its scope. The typical grievance award will deal with an individual grievant's complaint that he was discharged, laid off, or otherwise deprived of benefits or the opportunity to work, in violation of the existing management-union contract.

Almost a decade of experience under New York City's Interest Arbitration Statute reveals that "there has clearly been no chilling of the bargaining process" caused by the availability of arbitration as an alternate process, according to Arvid Anderson, the chairman of New York City's Office of Collective Bargaining.

Despite the classic apprehension about making arbitration the stand-in for bargaining, the New York City record presents a quite different perception of reality. As Anderson put it in his speech to a May 5, 1981, session of the National Academy of Arbitrators Annual Meeting in Maui, Hawaii:

> Contrary to predictions, there has been a very low utilization rate; only 8.6 percent of all contract disputes have required the use of impasse procedures. And more than half of that number represent awards which were the confirmation, in whole or in part, of the bargaining process of the parties.[135]

New York City's chief mediator also pointed to the near-absence of strikes under the interest arbitration law approved by the New York City Council in 1972. It became a part of the state's labor relations statutes for the public sector.

Since the enactment of the New York City law, there have been only three strikes over new contract terms. Nearly 600 individual contracts were negotiated during this period. There was a five-and-one-half-hour firefighter strike in 1973 which was settled by arbitration, a ten-day strike of off-track betting clerks in 1979 and a one-week strike of interns and residents in 1981 submitted to binding arbitration. In offering this favorable report card, Anderson also noted that collective bargaining — not interest arbitration — has been the prime process for setting the basic wage and benefit patterns in New York.

Interest arbitrations have concerned disputes where attempts were made to increase the basic wage pattern of the city or have involved special conditions of employment, such as whether or not one-man supervisory patrols should be implemented in the police department, or what the proper rate of compensation should be for two-man sanitation crews assigned to do the work previously performed by three-man crews.

Special stress must be given to the part of the record indicating that the interest arbitration awards have not exceeded the size of the negotiated settlements during the same period. The board has had to reduce an impasse panel's award in only two cases in nine years.

As mentioned, there were only two cases during the nearly ten-year period where the awards were found to be inconsistent with negotiated settlements. In the appellate process, these awards were reduced by the unanimous decisions of the tripartite board of collective bargaining to conform the awards to the city's basic wage patterns. It is also significant that less than one-fourth of all impasse panel awards have been appealed to the board of collective bargaining and that no awards have been successfully appealed to the courts.

Arbitration and Supreme Court Rulings

Three decisions handed down by the U.S. Supreme Court should spur employers and unions to draft specific contract language to protect against wildcat strikes, against individual litigation based upon statutory rights, and against charges of failure to represent.

The three rulings are *Complete Auto Transit, Inc., v. Reis* (107 LRRM 2145) holding that an employer may not collect damages against individual workers who violate a no-strike agreement by carrying out an unauthorized wildcat strike; *Barrentine v. Arkansas-Best Freight System* (24 WH cases 1284) allowing an employee to bring court action under the Fair Labor Standards Act even after denial of his grievance; and *Clayton v. UAW* and *ITT Gilfillan* (107 LRRM 2385) holding that a worker whose grievance is rejected does not have to exhaust the union's internal appeals before suing both the union and employer.

Each of these decisions weakens some aspect of collective bargaining. In all three cases litigation in the federal courts was preferred over the machinery selected by the union and the employer for settling their disputes. Justices Brennan, White, Marshall, Blackmun, and Stevens were in the majority on each occasion. The dissenting justices—Chief Justice Burger and Justice Rehnquist, sometimes joined by Justices Powell and Stewart—"pointed out the increasing pressure on the courts and the national policy in favor of contract grievance procedures as a preferred method for settling disputes."

Remedies for wildcat strikes. Turning to the specific cases, the remedies an employer has to deal with wildcat strikes are "illusory." Discharge is "seldom realistic," and wholesale discharges are impractical while elective discharges may be illegal. Injunctions against striking workers are generally prohibited, unions seldom discipline their striking workers, and employer suits for damages against unions are unlikely to succeed.

To remedy this problem, it is suggested the parties add new language to their grievance procedures: "For example, a specific reference to possible noncompliance by union members with the union's no-strike commitment may make a wildcat strike an arbitrable issue subject to injunction, damages and discharge sanctions."

Issues such as the minimum wage claim under Barrentine could be resolved by broadening an impartial arbitrator's authority to determine certain statutory questions plus an administrative practice of obtaining a grievant's written consent to having such matters submitted to arbitration. An arbitrator's power also could be expanded to include the broad range of relief that may be contained in the statute, sometime including the right to award actual and liquidated damages, reasonable attorney's fees and costs.

The joint grievance committee system of arbitration found in Teamster contracts "is so clearly defective as an impartial mechanism" that it is not surprising that we keep seeing it tested in the courts in cases such as Barrentine. I continue to be astonished that the Supreme Court refers to this system as "arbitration."

Grievance and arbitration procedures could incorporate a reference to an internal procedure by providing that the time limitation for filing a grievance for arbitration shall be tolled if a grievant makes use of available union procedures to seek review of a union decision not to proceed with the grievance. Unions concerned about "failure to represent" litigation could provide for impartial review and authorize an impartial tribunal to reactivate a grievance and send it to an arbitrator who would be authorized to grant the complete relief available by litigation.

If such changes in contract language were adopted at the bargaining table, the parties would be able to "respond to recent cases and to protect against a substantial amount of unnecessary litigation between union members and the contractual parties."

Other Issues. The balance between a union's desire for access to information and an employee's concern about disclosure is a "classic conflict between individual and group interests." An employer's refusal to give employee test scores to a union without the employee's consent was upheld by the Supreme Court in *Detroit Edison Company v. NLRB* (100 LRRM 2728), and a firm's refusal to give a union the names of employees with lung disease without the consent of those employees was approved by the board in *Johns Manville Sales Corporation v. Chemical Workers.* (105 LRRM 1379).

The balance between an employee's desire not to disclose information and the employer's desire to obtain information necessary for decisions often involves the controversial issue of truth verification with such methods as polygraph and voice stress tests.

The balance between employee access and an employer's desire to maintain confidentiality is tested when employees seek to correct historical data or to gain access to tests. The final issue involves the balance between the protection of personal privacy and government regulations and control of private information systems.

Arbitrators are reluctant to rely on polygraphs as evidence that employees are lying but will use such evidence as proof of innocence. Awards involving an employee's refusal to take a polygraph are "unclear and mixed." However, "the weight of arbitral authority appears to uphold discharge for employees who refuse" to submit to searches. This illustrates that arbitrators distinguish between "intellectual and physical privacy" and feel that intellectual privacy is entitled to greater protection.

Finality. While arbitral awards traditionally have been deemed final and binding, there have emerged two lines of cases that are exceptions. One involves the impact of external law such as the FLSA claim under Barrentine or the discrimination allegation under *Alexander v. Gardner-Denver.* (7FEP Cases 81).

Finality in arbitration is now "a much more tenuous concept" which is "going through a process of evolution" but the procedure will be strengthened with passage of time. To those who wonder whether to use arbitration when there is a possibility that a grievant also will seek to litigate, the answer clearly is yes. In the vast majority of cases arbitration will provide an end to the dispute; the handful of cases that go on to litigation are difficult to win.

Appendices

Examples of Shop Rules Forms

The following specimens of shop rules have been excerpted verbatim from various contracts. Identification has been supplied where it was available.

Specimen 1. Agreement between the Delco Radio Division of General Motors Corp. and the UAW.

Shop Rules. The purpose of these rules and regulations is not to restrict the rights of anyone, but to define them and protect the rights of all and insure cooperation.

Committing any of the following violations will be sufficient grounds for disciplinary action ranging from reprimand to immediate discharge, depending upon the seriousness of the offense in the judgment of management.

1. Falsification of personnel or other records.
2. Ringing the clock card of another.
3. Repeated failure to ring own card.
4. Using another's badge or pass, or permitting another to use your badge or pass to enter the property.
5. Failure to carry badge on your person at all times while on company premises.
6. Absence without reasonable cause.
7. Reporting late for work.
8. Absence of three working days without properly notifying management.
9. Leaving own department or the plant during working hours without permission.
10. Distracting the attention of others, or causing confusion by unnecessary shouting, catcalls or demonstration in the plant.
11. Littering or contributing to poor housekeeping [or] unsanitary or unsafe conditions on plant premises.
12. Possession of weapons on Company premises at any time.
13. Refusal to obey orders of foreman or other supervision.
14. Refusal or failure to do job assignment. (Do the work assigned to you and follow instructions; any complaint may be taken up later through the regular channels.)
15. Unauthorized operation of machines, tools or equipment.
16. Making scrap unnecessarily or careless workmanship.
17. Horseplay, scuffling, running or throwing things.
18. Wasting time or loitering in toilets or on any Company property during working hours.
19. Smoking except in specifically designated areas and during specified periods.

20. Threatening, intimidating, coercing or interfering with employees or supervision at any time.

21. Unauthorized soliciting or collecting contributions for any purpose whatsoever during working time.

22. Unauthorized distribution of literature, written or printed matter of any description in working areas on Company premises during working time.

23. Posting or removal of notices, signs or writing in any form on bulletin boards or Company property at any time without specific [authorization from] management.

24. Misuse or removal from the premises without proper authorization of employee lists, blueprints, Company records or confidential information of any nature.

25. Gambling [or playing a] lottery or any other game of chance on Company premises at any time.

26. Abuse, misuse or deliberate destruction of Company property, tools [or] equipment or the property of employees in any manner.

27. Restricting output.

28. The making or publishing of false, vicious or malicious statements concerning any employee, supervisor, the Company or its products.

29. Abusive language to any employee or supervision.

30. Fighting on the premises at any time.

31. Theft or misappropriation of property of employees or of the Company.

32. Possession of or drinking of liquor or any alcoholic beverage on Company property at any time. Reporting for work under [the] influence of alcohol, when suffering from alcoholic hangover, or in any unsafe condition.

33. Sabotage.

34. Disregard of safety rules or common safety practices.

35. Assignment of wages or frequent garnishments.

36. Immoral conduct or indecency.

37. Throwing refuse or objects on the floors or out the windows.

38. Stopping work or making preparations to leave work (such as washing up or changing clothes) before the signal sounds for lunch period or before the specified quitting time.

39. Repeated violations of shop or safety rules.

40. Failure to report all injuries, however small, to plant hospital. This applies to cuts, bruises, scratches, burns and all eye cases.

Specimen 2. Agreement between Samsonite Corporation and the URW.

Whereas all of the parties to the said collective bargaining agreement have agreed that, in consideration of the Employer executing the said collective bargaining agreement, the Union and the Employer would enter into a Supplemental Agreement setting forth the grounds for discharge or other disciplinary action.

Now, therefore, it is agreed between the parties as follows:

(a) Although the Employer may impose a lesser penalty, the following shall be just cause for immediate discharge.

1. Neglect of duty.

2. Dishonesty, including falsifying of the Employer's records of making false statements when applications for employment are being made.

3. Reporting for duty under the influence of intoxicating beverages or the use or possession of intoxicating beverages on Company property at any time.

4. Destruction, abuse, removal or attempted removal of the Employer's or another employee's property or materials.

5. Engaging in a strike, picketing, sabotage or slowdown or failure or refusal to cross a picket line at the premises of the Employer or at the premises of any of the Employer's customers in connection with their work.

6. Sleeping on the job.

7. Physical violence, fighting or creating a disturbance on the Employer's premises.

8. Possession of any weapon, as defined by law, on the Employer's premises.

9. Immoral or indecent conduct on the Employer's premises.

10. Conduct which violates the common decency or morality of the community.

11. Failure to report immediately accidents or personal injury to the proper authority.

12. Falsifying or refusing to give testimony when accidents or disciplinary actions are being investigated.

13. Failure of any employee to qualify for a surety bond or revocation by the surety company of any employee's coverage under a surety bond.

14. Insubordination, including refusal or failure to perform regular, Saturday, Sunday, holiday or overtime work duly assigned.

15. Disobedience of orders or acts of disrespect toward superiors.

16. Threatening, intimidating, coercing or abusing fellow employees, or any attempt to retard the work of fellow employees or otherwise disturb or interfere with them on the Employer's premises.

17. Lying to superiors in connection with their work.

18. Absence from work without receipt of proper notice by the Employer, unless failure to give such notice was due to circumstances beyond the control of the employee. The procedure for reporting absences from work is covered in a separate memorandum.

19. Absence from work where permission to be absent has not been given by the Employer, unless such absence is beyond the control of the employee.

20. Being late for work two (2) or more times in any thirty (30) day period without reasonable excuse.

21. Harboring a disease which may endanger the health of fellow employees.

22. Making disparaging remarks about the Employer or the products sold by the Employer or any words or deeds which would discourage any person from dealing with the Employer.

23. Prowling about the premises of the Employer without justifiable reason.

24. Changing assigned working places without permission.

25. Neglect in the care or use of the Employer's property.

26. Use of habit-forming drugs or narcotics or their introduction possession on the property of the Employer.

27. Abuse of break period.

28. Punching another employee's time card, or failure of an employee to properly punch his time card, during work hours.

29. Early punching of an employee's time card, or failure of an employee to properly punch his time card after work hours.

30. Improperly reporting piecework or incentive work, including the performance of any portion of a piecework or incentive job while on downtime or assisting, while on downtime, another employee who is working on a piecework or incentive basis.

31. Misuse or removal from the Employer's premises, without proper

authorization, of employee lists, Employer records, blueprints, or confidential information of any kind.

32. Unauthorized distribution of literature, written or printed matter on the Employer's premises, or posting or removing of notices, signs or writing in any form on bulletin boards or other proeprty of the Employer. However, employees may distribute Union literature on Company premises before or after work or during lunch or break periods, provided that the employee distributing the Union literature and the employee receiving the Union literature are both off work or on lunch or break periods at the time of the distribution.

33. Unauthorized operation or use of any machines, tools, equipment or other property of the Employer.

34. Negligence or carelessness resulting in damage or destruction to or loss of the Employer's property.

35. Failure to follow safety rules, or failure to use safety devices or appliances.

36. Unauthorized solicitations or collections for any pupose on the Employer's premises. However, solicitations of Union membership on Company premises are permissible before or after work or during break or lunch periods, provided that the employee doing the soliciting and the employee solicited are both off work or on break or lunch periods at the time of the solicitation.

37. Gambling or participation in games of chance on the Employer's premises.

38. Excessive absenteeism.

39. Tampering with or removing safety devices.

40. Any other act of dishonesty, gross misconduct, or gross neglect not listed above.

(b) Except as provided in paragraph (a), violation of the offenses listed below shall not be the cause for immediate discharge, but the offending employee shall be subject to a reprimand for a first offense, layoff up to five (5) working days for the second offense, and discharge for a third offense. For the purpose of this paragraph (b), ... at the end of each two (2) year period ... any warning slips issued by the Employer during said two (2) year period shall be disregarded. The employer may impose lesser penalties than those provided for in this paragraph (b) if he wishes. In [the] assessing [of] penalties, the second or third offense does not have to be the same type or kind as the first or second offense. The offenses which are subject to the said sequence of penalties shall include, but are not limited to, the following:

1. Reporting back to work late or stopping work early (lunch hour and rest periods included), or leaving own department before quitting time.

2. Failure or inability or lack of effort to perform work in accordance with recognized standards of performance, as to both quality and quantity.

3. Work of a personal nature, loitering, reading (other than in connection with the employee's job), visiting other departments without authorization, or other time wasting during working hours.

4. Engaging in horseplay, distracting [the] attention of others or creating disturbances, making derogatory statements to or concerning other employees, or unnecessary shouting, catcalls or demonstrations.

5. Smoking in unauthorized areas or during unauthorized times; wasting time or loitering in toilets or smoking rooms or elsewhere during working hours.

6. Creating or contributing to unsanitary or dirty conditions.

7. Absenteeism.

8. Lateness.

9. Loafing.

10. Uncooperative attitude.

11. Acts of disrespect toward customers or visitors on Employer's premises.

12. Garnishment or assignment of wages.

13. Working before a shift starts, after a shift ends, or during lunch or break periods.

14. Any other just cause.

(c) Failure of the Employer to enforce any of the provisions of this Supplemental Agreement in any one or more instances shall not be considered a waiver of any of the provisions of this Supplemental Agreement.

Specimen 3. Agreement between Mount Sinai Hospital, New York, N.Y., and Drug & Hospital Employees, AFL-CIO.

Employees are entitled to retain their jobs on the basis of good behavior, efficiency, and honesty. The Hospital shall have the right to discipline or discharge any employee who fails to meet the foregoing conditions, and particularly, but without limitation, offenses against Hospital discipline as listed in Appendix C, annexed to and made part of this Agreement.

Notwithstanding the provisions of Section C of this Article and Article XXII, a discharge or suspension based upon improper conduct of an employee towards a patient shall not be subject to the grievance and arbitration procedure. Should the Union claim, however, that an employee was discharged or suspended for reasons other than improper conduct of an employee towards patients, such latter issue, as distinguished from the question of improper conduct, may be submitted to the grievance and arbitration procedure.

Principal Offenses Against Hospital Discipline. The following list includes the principal offenses against Hospital discipline, as established by the Hospital. Punishment for these offenses shall range from verbal reprimand to dismissal:

1. Falsification of Employment Record or other Hospital records.

2. Failure to ring the time card, ringing another employee's time card, or permitting another employee to ring one's time card.

3. Unauthorized absence from post of duty during regular tour of duty.

4. Loafing or sleeping while on duty.

5. Refusal to follow instructions of the duly assigned supervisor; refusal to accept a job assignment; insubordination.

6. Use of vile, intemperate, or abusive language.

7. Immoral or illegal conduct.

8. Use of or unauthorized possession of intoxicating beverages on the Hospital's premises, or reporting to work under the influence of intoxicants.

9. Use of narcotics, except by prescription.

10. Threatening, intimidating, or coercing another employee.

11. Fighting, horseplay, annoying another employee, or other disorderly conduct on the Hospital's premises.

12. Possession of a weapon on the Hospital's premises.

13. Gambling, conducting games of chance, or possession of gambling devices on the Hospital's premises.

14. Creating unsafe or unsanitary conditions, or contributing to such conditions.

15. Smoking in unauthorized areas, or smoking at unauthorized times.

16. Unauthorized possession, use, copying, or reading of Hospital records, or disclosure of information contained in such records to unauthorized persons.
17. Larceny, misappropriation, or unauthorized possession or use of property belonging to the Hospital or to any employee, patient, or visitor.
18. Excessive absence or tardiness.
19. Negligence or deliberate destruction or misuse of Hospital property or property of another employee, patient or visitor.
20. Any willful act or conduct detrimental to patient care or Hospital operations.
21. Disregard concerning personal appearance, uniforms, dress, or personal hygiene.
22. Going to or being found in cafeteria, coffee shop, or snack bar at times other than those authorized.
23. Soliciting or accepting tips from patients, visitors, or staff.
24. Failure to render a personal service to any patient if such service is within the normal and usual scope of the employee's duties or is required by reason of an emergency relating to the patient.

Specimen 4. Agreement between Swan Rubber Division (Amerace ESNA Corp.) and the United Rubber Workers Union.

All infractions of Company rules, as shown in the Appendix hereto, [of] which official notice has been taken shall be noted by the Company in writing and shall become a part of the employee's service record, but only after a copy of the charge has been furnished to the employee who is accused. If the employee is later exonerated, such charge shall be stricken from the service record.

Notification of Conditions Which May Result in Reprimand.
1. Working time — Employees reporting for work shall be at their respective places of work at their scheduled starting time. They shall remain at work until their scheduled stopping time, except for brief necessary or excused absences.
2. Tardiness — Habitual tardiness will render an employee subject to a reprimand.

Notification of Conditions Which May Result in Suspension.
1. Multiple Reprimands — Any employee who receives three reprimands may be subject to suspension.
2. Defective Workmanship — Excessive waste of materials or continued defective workmanship.
3. Insubordination.

Notification of Conditions Which May Result in Discharge.
1. Multiple Reprimands — For the same offense.
2. Multiple Suspensions — For the same offense.
3. Misrepresentation — Employees misrepresenting material facts in obtaining employment with the Company shall be subject to dismissal. . . .

Specimen 5. Agreement involving the United Automobile, Aircraft and Agricultural Implement Workers of America.

Shop Rules and Penalties:
Reporting for work or working under the influence of liquor or having intoxicating liquors in possession. First offense — discharge.

Running through plant at any time except in emergencies. This includes entering or leaving the plant. First offense — warning; second offense — warning to three days off; third offense—one week off and sixty days' probation; fourth offense—discharge.

Horseplay. First offense—warning; second offense—one week off and sixty days' probation; third offense—discharge.

Loitering in rest rooms or in any other place where the employee's duties do not call for his presence. First offense—warning; second offense—warning and sixty days' probation; third offense—one week off and sixty days' probation; fourth offense—discharge.

Sleeping on duty. First offense—warning; second offense—discharge.

Failure to perform work as ordered. First offense—warning; second offense—one week off and sixty days' probation; third offense—discharge.

Conducting gambling devices, games, lotteries, punch boards, or bookmaking. First offense—warning; second offense—six days off; third offense—discharge.

Assault and assault and battery within the meaning of and as defined by the laws of the State of Michigan. First offense—one week off; second offense—discharge.

Stealing. First offense—discharge.

Carrying concealed firearms. First offense—discharge.

Habitual tardiness. First offense—warning; second offense—one week off and sixty days' probation; third offense—discharge.

Hoarding tools, gauges, or materials. First offense—warning; second offense—one week off and sixty days' probation; third offense—discharge.

Quitting work before proper time except when authorized by foreman or rules. First offense—warning; second offense—warning; third offense—one week off and sixty days' probation; fourth offense—discharge.

Tampering with or damaging equipment or gauges so as to produce scrap or hold up work. First offense—Company will report to Federal officials and discharge.

Any action, verbal or physical, on the part of any employee detrimental or disruptive to harmonious relations between employees. First offense—warning; second offense—one week off and sixty days' probation; third offense—discharge.

Conduct unbecoming to an employee and the making of vile, obscene, and provocative remarks. First offense—warning; second offense—three days off; third offense—one week off; fourth offense—discharge.

It will be necessary for every employee of this Company to wear a proper identification badge at all times while on Company property. When a man appears at work without his badge, he will either be given a temporary badge or [be] sent home after his badge, depending upon the circumstances of the case. An employee will be charged $.50 for each lost badge.

All employees leaving the plant before the end of a shift will [need] a pass from the foreman which is to be presented to the Plant Protection at the point of exit. The penalty for leaving without a pass will be ninety (90) days on probation and one week off during [those] ninety days, the week to be chosen by the Company some time during the probationary period.

It will be a violation of our posted rule on falsification of records for one employee to ring in or ring out another employee's time card.

Any employee leaving the plant or going to the office or other department on personal business must have a written pass from his foreman.

A package pass must be secured from the foreman to remove any property from the premises except lunch boxes and clothing belonging to employees.

If the physical condition of any employee is such that it may impair his own welfare or that of his fellow workers, he will not be permitted to work.

Specimen 6. Agreement involving the United Automobile, Aircraft and Agricultural Implement Workers of America.

Safety Rules. The prevention of accidents in this shop is one of your most important duties to yourself, to your family and to your fellow workers.

Fooling, scuffling or throwing "things" about the shop will not be tolerated.

The use of compressed air for any purpose other than that usually necessary for the performance of the work is strictly forbidden.

Goggles must be worn as instructed.

Loose clothing, rings and neckties are not to be worn around revolving machinery. Keep sleeves rolled up.

Shut down your machine when oiling, greasing, cleaning or repairing it, if necessary, in the interest of safety.

Electricity should not be fooled with. If there are any repairs or adjustments necessary, call for the electrician.

Guards and safety devices are always to be used and kept in place.

Report any dangerous conditions or defective machine to your foreman.

Do not touch a person who is operating a machine. If you wish to tell him something, wait until he has completed the piece or has stopped the machine.

Never leave a board with nails turned up. Turn them down or remove them.

In cases of injury in the shop, no matter how slight, be sure to receive treatment immediately at the First Aid Office.

Do not allow anyone but the First Aid Attendant to remove foreign bodies from your eyes or treat an eye injury. Blindness or serious infection often results from amateur treatment.

When an injury in the plant confines you to your home, notify the Company at once so that you may receive the proper attention.

Boeing Company Rules.

Appropriate disciplinary measures will be taken when an employee is determined by the Company to have committed any of the actions listed below, or when any employee engages in any practice which is inconsistent with ordinary, reasonable, common-sense rules of conduct.

Engaging in Un-American Activities.

Being a member of, or supporting by word, action, or association any organization that advocates the overthrow of the United States Government by force or by any illegal or unconstitutional methods. Violation of provisions of the espionage laws or regulations of the United States or any agency thereof.

Failure to Comply with Security and Fire Protection Regulations.

Violation of security provisions relating to the safeguarding of classified information. Entering or leaving Company premises by other than designated entrances and exits, or opening any exterior gates, doors, or exits where guards are not stationed. Failure to wear or improper display of identification badges. Lending or borrowing identification badges. Violation of Company traffic or parking regulations. Possession of weapons or explosives on Company premises without authorization. Possession of cameras on Company premises without authorization. Smoking in prohibited or hazardous areas.

Failure to Comply with Safety, Health or Environmental Regulations.

Failure of an employee to report any injury which he or she suffers or witnesses, any occurrences causing damage to Company or customer property or any violation of environmental protection regulations. Committing an act which could be detrimental to the safety or health of a fellow employee. Failure to comply with health and safety rules or with environmental protection procedures.

Dishonesty.

Theft or unauthorized possession of property belonging to the Company, Government, customer, vendor or another employee. False statements or intentional omissions. Unauthorized use of Company, Government, customer or vendor equipment, property, proprietary information, supplies or of Company time. Concealing defective work. Giving or taking gratuities or bribes. Intentionally punching the time card of a fellow employee or falsely reporting the attendance of another, or altering a time record.

Unacceptable Conduct or Performance.

Commission of a penal offense. Damaging or destroying Company, Government, vendor, employee or customer property through willfulness or negligence. Insubordination. Failure to accomplish assigned work in an efficient, satisfactory, acceptable manner. Fighting on Company premises or horse-play. Intimidation, harassment or coercion of fellow employee or customer, Government or vendor representatives. Gambling on Company premises. Uncivil, insulting, vile or obscene language or conduct. Interfering with production in any way. Entering Company premises under the influence of alcoholic beverages or drugs. Possession or consumption of alcoholic beverages or drugs on Company premises. Excessive garnishments. Littering. Soliciting contributions or sales without authorization, except solicitations during non-working times relating to union activities. Circulating or distributing petitions, handbills or other literature without authorization, except literature relating to union activities may be circulated in non-work areas during non-working time. Posting literature without authorization, except literature relating to union activities may be posted during non-working time on bulletin boards designated for employee use. (Union activities include any matters concerning the mutual aid and protection of employees protected by the National Labor Relations Act, as amended. Non-working time within the work period is defined as authorized paid break periods and authorized unpaid lunch periods.)

Neglect of Duty.

Misuse of Company time. Failure to punch time card or report time worked. Unacceptable attendance. Failure to observe assigned lunch schedule or shift starting and ending times.

Unauthorized Outside Interests or Employment.

Accepting other employment without prior approval while on leave of absence. Concealed interest or employment in outside business which adversely affects the Company or the employee's performance.

Examples of Special Clauses on Disciplinary Action and Discharges

The following specimens of clauses on disciplinary action and discharges have been excerpted verbatim from various contracts. Identification has been supplied where it was available.

Specimen 1. Agreement beween Johnson & Johnson and Textile Workers Union, AFL-CIO.

Discharge Subject to Grievance Procedure. The Employer shall have the right to suspend or to discharge employees. The Union shall have the right to take up any suspension or discharge case, except the suspension or discharge of a probationary employee, as a grievance within five (5) working days after such suspension or discharge takes place, and such case shall be subject to review under the grievance and arbitration procedure beginning at Step 3.

Specimen 2. Agreement between Carnegie-Illinois Steel Corp. and United Steelworkers of America, CIO.

Suspension Before Discharge — Grievance Procedure — Reinstatement with Back Pay After Unjustified Discharge. In the exercise of its rights as set forth in Section 10, Management agrees that an employee shall not be peremptorily discharged from and after the date hereof, but that in all instances in which Management may conclude that an employee's conduct may justify suspension or discharge, he shall be first suspended. Such initial suspension shall be for not more than five (5) calendar days. During this period of initial suspension the employee may, if he believes that he has been unjustly dealt with, request a hearing and a statement of the offense before his department head with or without an assistant grievance committeeman or grievance committeeman present as he may choose, or the General Superintendent, or the Manager of the Plant with or without the member or members of the grievance committee present, as he similarly may choose. At such hearing the facts concerning the case shall be made available to both parties. After such hearing or if no such hearing is requested Management may conclude whether the suspension shall be converted into a discharge or, dependent upon the facts of the case, that such suspension should be extended or revoked. If the suspension is revoked the employee shall be returned to employment and receive full compensation at his regular rate of pay for the time lost, but in the event a disposition shall result in either the affirmation or extension of the suspension or discharge of the employee, the employee may within five (5) calendar days after such disposition allege a grievance which shall be handled in accordance with the procedure of Section 9 — Adjustment of Grievances. Final decision on all suspension or discharge cases shall be made by the Company within five (5) calendar days from the date of filing of the grievance, if any. Should it be determined by the Company or in arbitration that the employee has been discharged or suspended unjustly, the Company shall reinstate the employee and pay full compensation at the employee's regular rate of pay for the time lost.

Specimen 3. Agreement between Otis Elevator Co. and Metropolitan Federation of Architects, Engineers, Chemists & Technicians, UOPWA, CIO.

Discharge for Unsatisfactory Work — Thirty-Day Warning. No employee covered by this Agreement shall be discharged for unsatisfactory work without first having received written warning as to his deficiency and a reasonable opportunity to improve his work, generally not less than thirty (30) working days. No warning need be given an employee before discharging him for any other proper cause.

Specimen 4. Agreement between United States Steel Corporation and United Steelworkers, AFL-CIO.

Suspension Before Discharge; Hearing and Presentation of Grievance; Reinstatement with Full Pay. An employee shall not be peremptorily discharged. In all cases in which Management may conclude that an employee's conduct may justify suspensions or discharge, he shall be suspended initially for not more than 5 calendar days, and given written notice of such action.... If such initial suspension is for 5 calendar days and if the employee affected believes that he has been unjustly dealt with, he mayu request and shall be granted, during this period, a hearing and a statement of the offense before a representative (status of department head or higher) designated by the General Superintendent of the plant with or without an assistant grievance committeeman or grievance committeeman present as the employee may choose.... In the event the suspension is affirmed, modified, extended, or converted into a discharge, the employee may, within 5 calendar days after notice of such action, file a grievance in the third step of the grievance procedure.... Should any initial suspension, or affirmation, modification, or extension thereof, or discharge be revoked by the Company, the Company shall reinstate and compensate the employee affected on the basis of an equitable lump sum payment mutually agreed to by the parties or, in the absence of agreement, make him whole in the manner set forth in Section 8-D below.

Specimen 5. Agreement involving the United Automobile, Aircraft and Agricultural Implement Workers of America, CIO.

(a) All disciplinary action shall be for cause. The Company agrees that it will notify the Union in writing of the reason for any disciplinary layoff or discharge and will also provide an opportunity for any employee laid off or discharged to contact his steward at a place in the plant designated by the Company, as soon as the employee has left his department.

(b) Any grievance involving a disciplinary layoff (but not a discharge) must be filed in writing on the standard grievance form with the Plant Superintendent within two working days of the notification of, or the taking of, the disciplinary layoff action, and shall be disposed of in accordance with the grievance procedure....

(c) In the event of a contemplated discharge the Company may lay off the employee, but as soon as discharge is proposed the Company shall notify him and the Chairman of the Plant Committee. Unless objection is filed by the employee or the Plant Committee with the Industrial Relations Department prior to the close of the second succeeding working day following such notification, the employee may be discharged at once or otherwise disciplined. Should objection be made, it shall be filed in writing on the standard grievance form and disposed of as a grievance under the grievance procedure....

(d) In the event that it shall be determined that any disciplinary layoff or discharge of any employee was unwarranted, the employee shall be reinstated without loss of seniority and given back pay for the time lost thereby in an amount equal to what he would have earned for the hours lost on the basis of his average earnings for the pay period immediately preceding the date of his layoff or discharge.

(2) In the event that [a] disciplinary layoff is made on a Sunday or a holiday forming the basis of a grievance by the Union and requiring the calling to the

plant of a steward, the time spent in handling the grievance by the steward on such Sunday or holiday shall be paid for aside from the time allowed and paid for under Section 2, Article II, hereof.

Specimen 6. Agreement involving International Association of Machinists, AFL.

After the 45-day probationary period, the Employer reserves to itself the unrestricted right to discharge an employee for just cause. It agrees, however, that except for theft, insubordination, habitual drunkenness, deliberate falsification of record of work performed, or willful injury to the Employer's property or to persons on its premises, it will not discharge an employee as herein defined for inefficiency or acts of omission or violations of the published Shop Rules unless such employee and the Shop Committee shall have been warned in writing that a repetition thereof or further or other violations of his duties as an employee will result in his discharge.

In the event an employee should be unjustly laid off or discharged, such employee shall be restored to service with rights unimpaired and paid for all time lost. Such employee shall be required to submit a written grievance within forty-eight (48) hours to [the] Shop Steward and such grievance to be settled as expeditiously as possible.

The term "discharge" does not include layoffs for the purpose of reducing the Employer's force of workmen.

Specimen 7. Agreement involving International Association of Machinists, AFL.

In the event that an employee is disciplined or discharged, he shall be given a plain and logical reason in writing for such action. If the employee is dissatisfied he must file a written complaint with the Company within twenty-four (24) hours from his dismissal. The Company and the Union shall jointly investigate the reasons for the dismissal and shall agree or disagree with the action by the Company within seventy-two (72) hours from the time of his dismissal. In the case of a disagreement within said time, the said parties shall agree upon a third disinterested person to investigate the dismissal, and the decision of any two shall be final and binding upon the employee and the parties hereto. The final decision must be rendered not later than one (1) week after the time of dismissal, and if the decision be that the dismissal was not justified, the employee shall be reinstated and reimbursed for loss of wages suffered by him. In no event shall any such employee be entitled to recover wages for more than three (3) weeks of five (5) days each, pending the final disposition of such investigation and complaint.

Specimen 8. Agreement between Overhead Door Corp. and United Brotherhood of Carpenters & Joiners, AFL-CIO.

Removal of Employee from Job for Unsatisfactory Production. When an employee does not meet the production quantity and quality standard as established for the particular job on which he is working, his foreman will make an effort to determine the reasons therefor and discuss the matter with the employee. A record shall be made of such effort and discussion which record shall be signed by the foreman and by the employee. If, as a result of and after such discussion, [the] standard is not then reached and there is a continued failure or refusal of the employee to meet the production standards, the same shall be considered due cause for discipline, and the Employer shall have the right to determine who should be disciplined in a group operation for failure of the group to meet production standards. If demotion or removal from the job is determined upon, the Employer may place the employee affected on any job which may be available within the capacities of the employee, and if there be no such available job then the employee shall be laid off to await an opening on an available job.

Specimen 9. Agreement between Carborundum Company and United Electrical Radio & Machine Workers.

The Company agrees that a member of the Union shall not be peremptorily discharged but that in all instances in which the Company may conclude that an employee's conduct may justify discharge, he shall first be suspended. This initial suspension shall not be for more than three (3) working days.

Upon being notified of the suspension it shall be the duty of the employee to leave his Department and go to the Personnel Office. The Chief Steward shall be notified immediately and be given the opportunity to review the case with the employee. At the conclusion of this meeting, the employee shall leave the plant, if it is impossible to schedule a meeting as outlined in Section 21 below.

During a period of initial suspension, the Union or the employee may, if it is believed that he has been unjustly dealt with, request a hearing before his foreman, the Personnel and/or the Plant Manager or his authorized representative, with the Chief Steward or any other Union representative present if the employee so desires.... If the suspension is revoked, the employee shall be returned to employment and will receive full compensation at his regular rate of pay for time lost; if the suspension is converted into discharge or disciplinary layoff the Union or the employee may, within five (5) working days after such disposition, file a protest with the Personnel Manager. In that event the matter will be disposed of promptly in the Grievance Procedure as outlined in Article VII of this Agreement and will be heard in the first instance in Step C, and where Step D is used special efforts will be made to expedite the case. If under that procedure it is agreed or decided that an injustice has been done, the action will be modified as may be necessary to correct the injustice, including where appropriate reinstatement and payment for time unjustly lost from work.

Specimen 10. Agreement between Doughnut Corp. of America and United Office and Professional Workers of America, CIO.

When an employee shall be dismissed or shall resign, the Employer shall, upon request of the employee, issue a true statement of his or her character and service; such statement shall not be used nor shall it be admissible at any hearing contesting such dismissal or in any litigation whatsoever.

Specimen 11. Agreement between Gardner-Denver Company and United Steelworkers of America.

Section 1. The Company retains the right to establish and enforce shop rules and regulations. It is understood that such rules and regulations will not impair or abridge the provisions of this Agreement. Violations of such rules and regulations may be cause for suspension or discharge.

Section 2. Rules and regulations governing employees covered by this

Agreement shall be discussed with the Union prior to their effectiveness. Any disciplinary action taken by the Company pursuant to such rules and regulations may be made the subject of a grievance.

Specimen 12. Agreement between the Great Western Sugar Company and Teamsters, Warehousemen and Sugar Workers.

Good cause for discipline or discharge of employees shall be in the Company's discretion. The Company shall furnish each discharged employee a copy of the Time Order indicating thereon the reason for his discharge. Any employee who believes that he has been unjustly disciplined or discharged may avail himself of the grievance procedure provided in this Article. Any employee who is found to have been unjustly disciplined or discharged shall be returned to his former status of employment and seniority.

Specimen 13. Agreement involving the United Automobile, Aircraft and Agricultural Implement Workers, CIO.

The Company agrees to post in each department a copy of general shop rules and regulations of the Company having plantwide effect, but these rules and regulations shall not be so devised as to abridge the rights of employees guaranteed by this Agreement. Any additions to or changes in such rules and regulations may be made either by adding to or [by] amending the regularly posted rules above mentioned or by posting special bulletins on Company bulletin boards. Such additions or changes to the rules and regulations shall be effective 48 hours after such addition, amendment or posting. Violation by any employee of shop rules or of any provisions of this Agreement shall be cause for discipline.

Specimen 14. Agreement involving the United Automobile, Aircraft and Agricultural Implement Workers, CIO.

It is mutually recognized that the maintenance of discipline is a function of Management. The disciplinary action should be for just cause. Cause for such action shall include the following: Repeated inadequate performance of work, breakage of equipment due to carelessness, reporting for work under the influence of liquor, repeated insubordination, conviction of a felony or any other act or action contrary to the benefit of the parties. Disciplinary action shall take the form of an immediate layoff not to exceed one calendar week, during which time the Company and the Bargaining Committee shall meet and make final disposition of the case. Any such decision reached shall be final.

Specimen 15. Agreement involving the United Automobile, Aircraft and Agricultural Implement Workers, CIO.

The Company will notify the chief steward of any disciplinary action that has been taken against any employee. Copies of all warnings presented to employees shall also be given to the chief steward. Any employee who claims he has been discharged without just cause may file a signed complaint with his foreman within 24 hours of his discharge and a copy with a member of the Bargaining Committee, and if he does so, the Bargaining Committee and a representative of Management with the employee's foreman will meet at once in respect to the claim. If the employee is upheld, the Company will reimburse him for his lost time. Before leaving the plant a discharged employee shall be entitled to interview his committeeman or his chief steward, if his committeeman or his chief steward is in the plant at the time, such interview to take place in the watchman's office.

Code of Professional Responsibility for Arbitrators of Labor–Management Disputes

As approved April 28, 1975, at the Annual Meeting of the National Academy of Arbitrators, Dorado Beach, Puerto Rico. The Code also was approved by the American Arbitration Association and Federal Mediation and Conciliation Service who are parties.

[Last amended May 29, 1985 at the NAA Annual Meeting
in Seattle, Wash.]

FOREWORD

This "Code of Professional Responsibility for Arbitrators of Labor-Management Disputes" is intended to supersede the "Code of Ethics and Procedural Standards for Labor-Management Arbitration," approved in 1951 by a Committee of the American Arbitration Association, by the National Academy of Arbitrators, and by representatives of the Federal Mediation and Conciliation Service (15 LA 961).

Revision of the 1951 Code was initiated officially by the same three groups in October 1972. The Joint Steering Committee named below was designated to draft a proposal.

Reasons for Code revision should be noted briefly. Ethical considerations and procedural standards are sufficiently intertwined to warrant combining the subject matter of Parts I and II of the 1951 Code under the caption of "Professional Responsibility." It has seemed advisable to eliminate admonitions to the parties (Part III of the 1951 Code) except as they appear incidentally in connection with matters primarily involving responsibilities of arbitrators. Substantial growth of third party participation in dispute resolution in the public sector requires consideration. It appears that arbitration of new contract terms may become more significant. Finally, during the interval of more than two decades, new problems have emerged as private sector grievance arbitration has matured and has become more diversified.

JOINT STEERING COMMITTEE
Chairman
   William E. Simkin
Representing American Arbitration Association
   Frederick H. Bullen
   Donald B. Straus
Representing Federal Mediation and Conciliation Service
   Lawrence B. Babcock, Jr.
   L. Lawrence Schultz
Representing National Academy of Arbitrators
   Sylvester Garrett
   Ralph T. Seward

PREAMBLE

Background

Voluntary arbitration rests upon the mutual desire of management and labor in each collective bargaining relationship to develop procedures for dispute settlement which meet their own particular needs and obligations. No two voluntary systems, therefore, are likely to be identical in practice. Words used to describe arbitrators (Arbitrator, Umpire, Impartial Chairman, Chairman of Arbitration Board, etc.) may suggest typical approaches but actual differences within any general type of arrangement may be as great as distinctions often made among the several types.

Some arbitration and related procedures, however, are not the product of voluntary agreement. These procedures, primarily but not exclusively applicable in the public sector, sometimes utilize other third party titles (Fact Finder, Impasses Panel, Board of Inquiry, etc.). These procedures range all the way from arbitration prescribed by statute to arrangements substantially indistinguishable from voluntary procedures.

The standards of professional responsibility set forth in this Code are designed to guide the impartial third party serving in these diverse labor-management relationships.

Scope of Code

This Code is a privately developed set of standards of professional behavior. It applies to voluntary arbitration of labor-management grievance disputes and of disputes concerning new or revised contract terms. Both "ad hoc" and "permanent" varieties of voluntary arbitration, private and public sector, are included. To the extent relevant in any specific case, it also applies to ad-visory arbitration, impasses resolution panels, arbitration prescribed by statutes, fact-finding, and other special procedures.

The word "arbitrator," as used hereafter in the Code, is intented to apply to any impartial person, irrespective of specific title, who serves in a labor-management disputes procedure in which there is conferred authority to decide issue or to make formal recommendations.

The Code is not designed to apply to mediation or conciliation, as distinguished from arbitration, not to other procedures in which the third party is not authorized in advance to make decisions or recommendations. It does not apply to partisan representatives on tripartite boards. It does not apply to commercial arbitration or to other uses of arbitration outside the labor-management dispute area.

Format of Code

Bold Face type, sometimes including explanatory material, is used to set forth general principles. *Italics* are used for amplification of general principles. Ordinary type is used primarily for illustrative or explanatory comment.

Application of Code

Faithful adherence by an arbitrator to this Code is basic to professional responsibility.

The National Academy of Arbitrators will expect its members to be governed in their professional conduct by this Code and stands ready, through its Committee on Ethics and Grievances, to advise its members as to the Code's interpretation. The American Arbitration Association and the Federal Mediation and Conciliation Service will apply the Code to the arbitrators on their rosters in cases handled under their respective appointment or referral procedures. Other arbitrators and administrative agencies may, of course, voluntarily adopt the Code and be governed by it.

In interpreting the Code and applying it to charges of professional misconduct, under existing or revised procedures of the National Academy of Arbitrators and of the administrative agencies, it should be recognized that while some of its standards express ethical principles basic to the arbitration profession, others rest less on ethics than on considerations of good practice. Experience has shown the difficulty of drawing rigid lines of distinction between ethics and good practice and this Code does not attempt to do so. Rather, it leaves the gravity of alleged misconduct and the extent to which ethical standards have been violated to be assessed in the light of the facts and circumstances of each particular case.

I. ARBITRATOR'S QUALIFICATIONS AND RESPONSIBILITIES TO THE PROFESSION

A. *General Qualifications*

1. Essential personal qualifications of an arbitrator include honesty, integrity, impartiality and general competence in labor relations matters.

An arbitrator must demonstrate ability to exercise these personal qualities faithfully and with good judgment, both in procedural matters and in substantive decisions.

a. Selection by mutual agreement of the parties or direct designation by an administrative agency are the effective methods of appraisal of this combination of an individual's potential and performance, rather than the fact of placement on a roster of an administrative agency or membership in a professional association of arbitrators.

2. An arbitrator must be as ready to rule for one party as for the other on each issue, either in a single case or in a group of cases. Compromise by an arbitrator for the sake of attempting to achieve personal acceptability is unprofessional.

B. *Qualifications for Special Cases*

1. An arbitrator must decline appointment, withdraw, or request technical assistance when he or she decides that a case is beyond his or her competence.

a. An arbitrator may be qualified generally but not for specialized assignments. Some types of incentive, work standard, job evaluation, welfare program, pension, or insurance cases may require specialized knowledge, experience or competence. Arbitration of contract terms also may require distinctive background and experience.

b. Effective appraisal by an administrative agency or by an arbitrator of the need for special qualifications requires that both parties make known the special nature of the case prior to appointment of the arbitrator.

C. *Responsibilities to the Profession*

1. An arbitrator must uphold the dignity and integrity of the office and endeavor to provide effective service to the parties.

a. To this end, an arbitrator should keep current with principles, practices and developments that are relevant to his or her own field of arbitration practice.

2. An experienced arbitrator should cooperate in the training of new arbitrators.

3. An arbitrator must not advertise or solicit arbitration assignments.

a. It is a matter of personal preference whether an arbitrator includes "Labor Arbitrator" or similar notation on letterheads, cards, or announcements. *It is inappropriate, however, to include memberships or offices held in professional societies or listings on rosters of administrative agencies.*

b. Information provided for published biographical sketches, as well as that supplied to administrative agencies, must be accurate. Such information may include membership in professional organizations (including reference to significant offices held), and listings on rosters of administrative agencies.

II. RESPONSIBILITIES TO THE PARTIES

A. Recognition of Diversity in Arbitration Arrangements

1. An arbitrator should conscientiously endeavor to understanding and observe, to the extent consistent with professional responsibility, the significant principles governing each arbitration system in which he or she serves.

a. Recognition of special features of a particular arbitration arrangement can be essential with respect to procedural matters and may influence other aspects of the arbitration process.

2. Such understanding does not relieve an arbitrator from a corollary responsibility to seek to discern and refuse to lend approval or consent to any collusive attempt by the parties to use arbitration for an improper purpose.

B. Required Disclosures

1. Before accepting an appointment, an arbitrator must disclose directly or through the administrative agency involved, any current or past managerial, representational, or consultative relationship with any company or union involved in a proceeding in which he or she is being considered for appointment or has been tentatively designated to serve.

Disclosure must also be made of any pertinent pecuniary interest.

a. The duty to disclose includes membership on a Board of Directors, full-time or part-time service as a representative or advocate, consultation work for a fee, current stock or bond ownership (other than mutual fund shares or appropriate trust arrangements) or any other pertinent form of managerial, financial or immediate family interests in the company or union involved.

2. When an arbitrator is serving concurrently as an advocate for or representative of other companies or unions in labor relations matters, or has done so in recent years, he or she must disclose such activities before accepting appointment as an arbitrator.

An arbitrator must disclose such activities to an administrative agency if he or she is on that agency's active roster or seeks placement on a roster. Such disclosure then satisfies this requirement for cases handled under that agency's referral.

a. It is not necessary to disclose names of clients or other specific details. It is necessary to indicate the general nature of the labor relations advocacy or representational work involved, whether for companies or unions or both, and a reasonable approximation of the extent of such activity.

b. An arbitrator on an administrative agency's roster has a continuing obligation to notify the agency of any significant changes pertinent to this requirement.

c. When an administrative agency is not involved, an arbitrator must make such disclosure directly unless he or she is certain that both parties to the case are fully aware of such activities.

3. An arbitrator must not permit personal relationships to affect decision-making.

Prior to acceptance of an appointment, an arbitrator must disclose to the parties or to the administrative agency involved any close personal relationship or other circumstance, in addition to those specifically mentioned earlier in this section, which might reasonably raise a question as to the arbitrator's impartiality.

a. Arbitrators establish personal relationships with many company and union representatives, with fellow arbitrators, and with fellow members of various professional associations. There should be no attempt to be secretive about such friendships or acquaintances but disclosure is not necessary unless some feature of a particular relationship might reasonably appear to impair impartiality.

4. If the circumstances requiring disclosure are not known to the arbitrator prior to acceptance of appointment, disclosure must be made when such circumstances become known to the arbitrator.

5. The burden of disclosure rests on the arbitrator. After appropriate disclosure, the arbitrator may serve if both parties so desire. If the arbitrator believes or perceives that there is a clear conflict of interest, he or she should withdraw, irrespective of the expressed desires of the parties.

C. Privacy of Arbitration
1. All significant aspects of an arbitration proceeding must be treated by the arbitrator as confidential unless this requirement is waived by both parties or disclosure is required or permitted by law.

a. Attendance at hearings by persons not representing the parties or invited by either or both of them should be permitted only when the parties agree or when an applicable law requires or permits. Occasionally, special circumstances may require

than an arbitration rule on such matters as attendance and degree of participation of counsel selected by a grievant.

b. Discussion of a case at any time by an arbitrator with persons not involved directly should be limited to situations where advance approval or consent of both parties is obtained or where the identity of the parties and details of the case are sufficiently obscured to eliminate any realistic probability of identification.

A commonly recognized exception is discussion of a problem in a case with a fellow arbitrator. *Any such discussion does not relieve the arbitrator who is acting in the case from sole responsibility for the decision and the discussion must be considered as confidential.*

Discussion of aspects of a case in a classroom without prior specific approval of the parties is not a violation provided the arbitrator is satisfied that there is no breach of essential confidentiality.

c. It is violation of professional responsibility for an arbitrator to make public an award without the consent of the parties.

An arbitrator may ask the parties whether they consent to the publication of the award either at the hearing or at the time the award is issued.

(1) If such question is asked at the hearing it should be asked in writing as follows:

"Do you consent to the submission of the award in this matter for publication?

(   )   (   )
YES   NO

If you consent you have the right to notify the arbitrator within 30 days after the date of the award that you revoke your consent."

It is desirable but not required that the arbitrator remind the parties at the time of the issuance of the award of their right to withdraw their consent to publication.

(2) If the question of consent to the publication of the award is raised at the time the award is issued, the arbitrator may state in writing to each party that failure to answer the inquiry within 30 days will be considered an implied consent to publish.

d. It is not impoper for an arbitrator to donate arbitration files to a library of a college, university or similar institution without prior consent of all the parties involved. When the circumstances permit, there should be deleted from such donations any cases concerning which one or both of the parties have expressed a desire for privacy. As an additional safeguard, an arbitrator may also decide to withhold recent cases or indicate to the donee a time interval before such cases can be made generally available.

e. Applicable laws, regulations, or practice of the parties may permit or even require exceptions to the above noted principles of privacy.

D. Personal Relationships with the Parties

1. An arbitrator must make every reasonable effort to conform to arrangements required by an administrative agency or mutually desired by the parties regarding communications and personal relationships with the parties.

a. Only an "arm's length" relationship may be acceptable to the parties in some arbitration arrangements or may be required by the rules of an administrative agency. The arbitrator should then have no contact of consequence with representatives of either party while handling a case without the other party's presence or consent.

*b. In other situations, both parties may want communications and personal relationships to be less for-*mal. It is then appropriate for the arbitrator to respond accordingly.*

E. Jurisdiction

1. An arbitrator must observe faithfully both the limitations and inclusions of the jurisdiction conferred by an agreement or other submission under which he or she serves.

2. A direct settlement by the parties of some or all issues in a case, at any stage of the proceedings, must be accepted by the arbitrator as relieving him or her of further jurisdiction over such issues.

F. Mediation by an Arbitrator

1. When the parties wish at the outset to give an arbitrator authority both to mediate and to decide or submit recommendations regarding residual issues, if any, they should so advise the arbitrator prior to appointment. If the appointment is accepted, the arbitrator must perform a mediation role consistent with the circumstances of the case.

a. Direct appointments, also, may require a dual role as mediator and arbitrator of residual issues. This is most likely to occur in some public sector cases.

2. When a request to mediate is first made after appointment, the arbitrator may either accept or decline a mediation role.

a. Once arbitration has been invoked, either party normally has a right to insist that the process be continued to decision.

b. If ony party requests that the arbitrator mediate and the other party objects, the arbitrator should decline the request.

c. An arbitrator is not precluded from making a suggestion that he or she mediate. To avoid the possibility of improper pressure, the arbitrator should not so suggest unless it can be discerned that both parties are likely to be receptive. In any event, the arbitrator's suggestion should not be pursued unless both parties agree.

G. Reliance by an Arbitrator on Other Arbitration Awards or on Independent Research

1. An arbitrator must assume full personal responsibility for the decision in each case decided.

a. The extent, if any, to which an arbitrator properly may rely on precedent, on guidance of other awards, or on independent research is dependent primarily on the policies of the parties on these matters, as expressed in the contract, or other agreement, or at the hearing.

b. When the mutual desires of the parties are not known or when the parties express differing opinions or policies, the arbitrator may exercise discretion as to these matters, consistent with the acceptance of full personal responsibility for the award.

H. Use of Assistants

1. An arbitrator must not delegate any decision-making function to another person without consent of the parties.

a. Without prior consent of the parties, an arbitrator may use the services of an assistant for research, clerical, duties, or preliminary drafting under the direction of the arbitrator which does not involve the delegation of any decision-making function.

b. If an arbitrator is unable, because of time limitations or other reasons, to handle all decision-making aspects of a case, it is not a violation of professional responsibility to suggest to the parties an allocation of responsibility between the arbitrator and an assistant or associate. The arbitrator must not exert pressure on the parties to accept such a suggestion.

I. Consent Awards

1. Prior to issuance of an award, the parties may jointly request the arbitrator to include in the award certain agreements between them, concerning some or all of the issues. If the arbitrator believes that a suggested award is proper, fair, sound, and lawful, it is consistent with professional responsibility to adopt it.

a. Before complying with such a request, an arbitrator must be certain that he or she understands the suggested settlement adequately in order to be able to appraise its terms. If it appears that pertinent facts or circumstances may not have been disclosed the arbitrator should take the initiative to assure that all significant aspects of the case are fully understood. To this end, the arbitrator may request additional specific information and may question witnesses at a hearing.

J. Avoidance of Delay

It is a basic professional responsibility of an arbitrator to plan his or her work schedule so that present and future commitments will be fulfilled in a timely manner.

a. When planning is upset for reasons beyond the control of the arbitrator, he or she, nevertheless, should exert every reasonable effort to fulfill all commitments. If this is not possible, prompt notice at the arbitrator's initiative should be given to all parties affected. Such notices should include reasonably accurate estimates of any additional time required. To the extent possible, priority should be given to cases in process so that other parties may make alternative arbitration arrangements.

2. An arbitrator must cooperate with the parties and with any administrative agency involved in avoiding delays.

a. An arbitrator on the active roster of an administrative agency must take the initiative in advising the agency of any scheduling difficulties that he or she can foresee.

b. Requests for services, whether received directly or through an administrative agency, should be declined if the arbitrator is unable to schedule a hearing as soon as the parties wish. If the parties, nevertheless, jointly desire to obtain the services of the arbitrator and the arbitrator agrees arrangements should be made by agreement that the arbitrator confidently expects to fulfill.

c. An arbitrator may properly seek to persuade the parties to alter or eliminate arbitration procedures or tactics that cause unnecessary delay.

3. Once the case record has been closed, an arbitrator must adhere to the time limits for an award, as stipulated in the labor agreement or as provided by regulation of an administrative agency or as otherwise agreed.

a. If an appropriate award cannot be rendered within the required time, it is incumbent on the arbitrator to seek an extension of time from the parties.

b. If the parties have agreed upon abnormally short time limits for an award after a case is closed, the arbitrator should be so advised by the parties or by the administrative agency involved, prior to acceptance of appointment.

K. Fees and Expenses

1. An arbitrator occupies a position of trust in respect to the parties and the administrative agencies. In charging for services and expenses the arbitrator must be governed by the same high standards of honor and integrity that apply to all other phases of his or her work.

An arbitrator must endeavor to keep total charges for services and expenses reasonable and consistent with the nature of the case or cases decided.

Prior to appointment, the parties should be aware of or be able readily to determine all significant aspects of an arbitrator's bases for charges for fees and expenses.

a. Services Not Primarily Chargeable on a Per Diem Basis

By agreement with the parties, the financial aspects of many "permanent" arbitration assignments, of some interest disputes, and of some "ad hoc" grievance assignments do not include a per diem fee for services as a primary part of the total understanding. *In such situations, the arbitrator must adhere faithfully to all agreed upon arrangements governing fees and expenses.*

b. Per Diem Basis for Charges for Services

(1) *When an arbitrator's charges for services are determined primarily by a stipulated per diem fee, the arbitrator should establish in advance his or her bases for application of such per diem fee and for determination of reimbursable expenses.*

Practices established by an arbitrator should include the basis for charges, if any, for:

(a) hearing time, including the arbitration of the stipulated basic per diem hearing fee to hearing days of varying lengths;

(b) study time;

(c) necessary travel time when not included in charges for hearing time;

(d) postponement or cancellation of hearings by the parties and the circumstances in which such charges will normally be assessed or waived;

(e) office overhead expenses (secretarial, telephone, postage, etc.);

(f) the work of paid assistants or associates.

(2) *Each arbitrator should be guided by the following general principles:*

(a) Per diem charges for a hearing should not be in excess of actual

time spent or allocated for the hearing.

(b) Per diem charges for study time should not be in excess of actual time spent.

(c) any fixed ratio of study days to hearing days, not agreed to specifically by the parties, is inconsistent with the per diem method of charges for services.

(d) Charges for expenses must not be in excess of actual expenses normally reimbursable and incurred in connection with the case or cases involved.

(e) When time or expense are involved for two or more sets of parties on the same day or trip, such time or expense charges should be approximately prorated.

(f) An arbitrator may stipulate in advance a mnimum charge for a hearing without violation of (a) or (e) above.

(3) An arbitrator on the active roster of an administrative agency must file with the agency his or her individual bases for determination of fees and expenses if the agency so requires. Thereafter, it is the responsibility of each such arbitrator to advise the agency promptly of any change in any basis for charges.

Such filing may be in the form of answers to a questionnaire devised by an agency or by any other method adopted by or approved by an agency.

Having supplied an administrative agency with the information noted above, an arbitrator's professional responsibility of disclosure under this Code with respect to fees and expenses has been satisfied for cases referred by that agency.

(4) If an administrative agency promulgates specific standards with respect to any of these matters which are in addition to or more restrictive than an individual arbitrator's standards, an arbitrator on its active

roster must observe the agency standards for cases handled under the auspices of that agency or decline to serve.

(5) When an arbitrator is contracted directly by the parties for a case or cases, the arbitrator has a professional responsibility to respond to questions by submitting his or her bases for charges for fees and expenses.

(6) When it is known to the arbitrator that one or both of the parties cannot afford normal charges, it is consistent with professional responsibility to charge lesser amounts to both parties or to one of the parties if the other party is made aware of the difference and agrees.

(7) If an arbitrator concludes that the total of charges derived from his or her normal basis of calculation is not compatible with the case decided, it is consistent with professional responsibility to charge lesser amounts to both parties.

2. An arbitrator must maintain adequate records to support charges for services and expenses and must make an accounting to the parties or to an involved administrative agency on request.

III. RESPONSIBILITIES TO ADMINISTRATIVE AGENCIES

A. General Responsibilities

1. An arbitrator must be candid, accurate, and fully responsive to an administrative agency concerning his or her qualifications, availability, and all other pertinent matters.

2. An arbitrator must observe policies and rules of an administrative agency in cases referred by that agency.

3. An arbitrator must not seek to influence an administrative agency by any improper means, including gifts or other inducements to agency personnel.

a. It is not improper for a person seeking placement on a roster to request references from individuals having knowledge of the applicant's experience and qualifications.

b. Arbitrators should recognize that the primary responsibility of an administrative agency is to serve the parties.

IV. PREHEARING CONDUCT

1. All prehearing matters must be handled in a manner that fosters complete impartiality by the arbitrator.

a. The primary purpose of prehearing discussions involving the arbitrator is to obtain agreement on procedural matters so that the hearing can proceed without unnecessary obstacles. If differences of opinion should arise during such discussions and particularly, if such differences appear to impinge on substantive matters, the circumstances will suggest whether the matter can be resolved informally or may require a prehearing conference or, more rarely, a formal preliminary hearing. When an administrative agency handles some or all aspects of the arrangements prior to a hearing, the arbitrator will become involved only if differences of some substance arise.

b. Copies of any prehearing correspondence between the arbitrator and either party must be made available to both parties.

V. HEARING CONDUCT

A. General Principles

1. An arbitrator must provide a fair and adequate hearing which assures that both parties have sufficient opportunity to present their respective evidence and argument.

a. Within the limits of this responsibility, an arbitrator should conform to the various types of hearing procedures desired by the parties.

b. An arbitrator may: encourage stipulations of fact; restate the substance of issues or arguments to promote or certify understanding; question the parties' representatives or witnesses, when necessary or advisable, to obtain additional pertinent information; and request that the parties submit additional evidence, either at the hearing or by subsequent filing.

c. An arbitrator should not intrude into a party's presentation so as to prevent that party from putting forward its case fairly and adequately.

B. Transcripts or Recordings

1. Mutual agreement of the parties as to use or non-use of a transcript must be respected by the arbitrator.

a. A transcript is the official record of a hearing only when both parties agree to a transcript or an applicable law or regulation so provides.

b. An arbitrator may seek to persuade the parties to avoid use of a transcript, or to use a transcript if the nature of the case appears to require one. *However, if an arbitrator intends to make his or her appointment to a case contingent on mutual agreement to a transcript, that requirement must be made known to both parties prior to appointment.*

c. If the parties do not agree to a transcript, an arbitrator may permit one party to take a transcript at its own cost. The arbitrator may also make appropriate arrangements under which the other party may have access to a copy if a copy is provided to the arbitrator.

d. Without prior approval, an arbitrator may seek to use his or her own tape recorder to supplement note taking. The arbitrator should not insist on such a tape recording if either or both parties object.

C. *Ex Parte Hearings*

1. In determining whether to conduct an ex parte hearing, an arbitrator must consider relevant legal, contractual, and other pertinent circumstances.

2. An arbitrator must be certain, before proceeding ex parte, that the party refusing or failing to attend the hearing has been given adequate notice of the time, place and purposes of the hearing.

D. *Plant Visits*

1. An arbitrator should comply with a request of any party that he or she visit a work area pertinent to the dispute prior to, during, or after a hearing. An arbitrator may also initiate such a request.

a. Procedures for such visits should be agreed to by the parties in consultation with the arbitrator.

E. *Bench Decisions or Expedited Awards*

1. When an arbitrator understands, prior to acceptance of appointment, that a bench decision is expected at the conclusion of the hearing, the arbitrator must comply with the understanding unless both parties agree otherwise.

a. If notice of the parties' desire for a bench decision is not given prior to the arbitrator's acceptance of the case, issuance of such a bench decision is discretionary.

b. When only one party makes the request and the other objects, the arbitrator should not render a bench decision except under most unusual circumstances.

2. When an arbitrator understands, prior to acceptance of appointment, that a concise written award is expected within a stated time period after the hearing, the arbitrator must comply with the understanding unless both parties agree otherwise.

VI. POST HEARING CONDUCT

A. *Post Hearing Briefs and Submissions*

1. An arbitrator must comply with mutual agreements in respect to the filing or nonfiling of post hearing briefs or submissions.

a. An arbitrator, in his or her discretion, may either suggest the filing of post hearing briefs or other submissions or suggest that none be filed.

b. When the parties disagree as to the need for briefs, an arbitrator may permit filing but may determine a reasonable time limitation.

2. An arbitrator must not consider a post hearing brief or submission that has not been provided to the other party.

B. *Disclosure of Terms of Award*

1. An arbitrator must not disclose a prospective award to either party prior to its simultaneous issuance to both parties or explore possible alternative awards unilaterally with one party, unless both parties so agree.

a. Partisan members of tripartite boards may know prospective terms of an award in advance of its issuance. Similar situations may exist in other less formal arrangements mutually agreed to by the parties. In any such situation, the arbitrator should determine and observe the mutually desired degree of confidentiality.

C. *Awards and Opinions*

1. The award should be definite, certain and as concise as possible.

a. When an opinion is required, factors to be considered by an arbitrator include: desirability of brevity, consistent with the nature of the case and any expressed desires of the parties; need to use a style and form that is understandable to responsible representatives of the parties, to the grievant and supervisors, and to others in the collective bargaining relationships; necessity of meeting the significant issues; forthrightness to an extent not harmful to the relationship of the parties; and avoidance of gratuitous advice or discourse not essential to disposition of the issues.

D. Clarification or Interpretation of Awards

1. No clarification or interpretation of an award is permissible without the consent of both parties.

2. Under agreements which permit or require clarification or interpretation of an award, an arbitrator must afford both parties an opportunity to be heard.

E. Enforcement of Award

1. The arbitrator's responsibility does not extend to the enforcement of an award.

2. In view of the professional and confidential nature of the arbitration relationship, an arbitrator should not voluntarily participate in legal enforcement proceedings.

American Arbitration Association
Voluntary Labor Arbitration Rules

(As amended and in effect February 1, 1987)

1. Agreement of Parties – The parties shall be deemed to have made these rules a part of their arbitration agreement whenever, in a collective bargaining agreement or Submission, they have provided for arbitration by the American Arbitration Association (hereinafter AAA) or under its rules. These rules shall apply in the form obtaining at the time the arbitration is initiated.

2. Name of Tribunal – Any tribunal constituted by the parties under these rules shall be called the Voluntary Labor Arbitration Tribunal.

3. Administrator – When parties agree to arbitrate under these Rules and an arbitration is instituted thereunder, they thereby authorize the AAA to administer the arbitration. The authority and obligations of the administrator are as provided in the agreement of the parties and in these rules.

4. Delegation of Duties – The duties of the AAA may be carried out through such representatives or committees as the AAA may direct.

5. National Panel of Labor Arbitrators – The AAA shall establish and maintain a National Panel of Labor Arbitrators and shall appoint arbitrators therefrom, as hereinafter provided.

6. Office of Tribunal – The general office of the Voluntary Labor Arbitration Tribunal is the headquarters of the AAA, which may, however, assign the administration of an arbitration to any of its regional offices.

7. Initiation Under an Arbitration Clause in a Collective Bargaining Agreement – Arbitration under an arbitration clause in a collective bargaining agreement under these rules may be initiated by either party in the following manner:

(a) By giving written notice to the other party of intention to arbitrate (Demand), which notice shall contain a statement setting forth the nature of the dispute and the remedy sought, and

(b) By filing at any regional office of the AAA three copies of said notice, together with a copy of the collective bargaining agreement, or such parts thereof as relate to the dispute, including the arbitration provisions. After the Arbitrator is appointed, no new or different claim may be submitted except with the consent of the Arbitrator and all other parties.

8. Answer — The party upon whom the Demand for arbitration is made may file an answering statement with the AAA within seven days after notice from the AAA, simultaneously sending a copy to the other party. If no answer is filed within the stated time, it will be assumed that the claim is denied. Failure to file an answer shall not operate to delay the arbitration.

9. Initiation Under a Submission — Parties to any collective bargaining agreement may initiate an arbitration under these rules by filing at any regional office of the AAA two copies of a written agreement to arbitrate under these rules (Submission), signed by the parties and setting forth the nature of the dispute and the remedy sought.

10. Fixing of Locale — The parties may mutually agree upon the locale where the arbitration is to be held. If the locale is not designated in the collective bargaining agreement or Submission, and if there is a dispute as to the appropriate locale, the AAA shall have the power to determine the locale and its decision shall be binding.

11. Qualifications of an Arbitrator — No person shall serve as a neutral arbitrator in any arbitration in which he or she has any financial or personal interest in the result of the arbitration, unless the parties, in writing, waive such disqualification.

12. Appointment from Panel — If the parties have not appointed an arbitrator and have not provided any other method of appointment, the arbitrator shall be appointed in the following manner: Immediately after the filing of the Demand or Submission, the AAA shall submit simultaneously to each party an identical list of names of persons chosen from the National Panel of Labor Arbitrators. Each party shall have seven days from the mailing date in which to cross off any names to which it objects, number the remaining names to indicate the order of preference, and return the list to the AAA. IF a party does not return the list within the time specified, all persons named therein shall be deemed acceptable. From among the persons who have been approved on both lists, and in accordance with the designated order of mutual preference, the AAA shall invite the acceptance of an arbitrator to serve. If the parties fail to agree upon any of the persons named, if those named decline or are unable to act, or if for any other reason the appointment cannot be made from the submitted lists, the administrator shall have the power to make the appointment from other members of the Panel without the submission of any additional list.

13. Direct Appointment by Parties — If the agreement of the parties names an arbitrator or specifies a method of appointing an arbitrator, that designation or method shall be followed. The notice of appointment, with the name and address of such arbitrator, shall be filed with the AAA by the appointing party.

If the agreement specifies a period of time within which an arbitrator shall be appointed, and any party fails to make such appointment within that period, the AAA may make the appointment.

If no period of time is specified in the agreement, the AAA shall notify the parties to make the appointment and if within seven days thereafter such arbitrator has not been so appointed, the AAA shall make the appointment.

14. Appointment of Neutral Arbitrator by Party-Appointed Arbitrators — If the parties have appointed their arbitrators, or if either or both of them have been appointed as provided in Section 13, and have authorized such arbitrators to appoint a neutral arbitrator within a specified time and no appointment is made within such time or any agreed extension thereof, the AAA may appoint a neutral arbitrator, who shall act as chairperson.

If no period of time is specified for appointment of the neutral arbitrator and the parties do not make the appointment within seven days from the date of the appointment of the last party-appointed arbitrator, the AAA shall appoint such neutral arbitrator, who shall act as chairperson.

If the parties have agreed that the arbitrators shall appoint the neutral arbitrator from the panel, the AAA shall furnish to the party-appointed arbitrators, in the manner prescribed in Section 12, a list selected from the panel, and the appointment of the neutral arbitrator shall be made as prescribed in that Section.

15. Number of Arbitrators — If the arbitration agreement does not specify the number of arbitrators, the dispute shall be heard and determined by one arbitrator, unless the parties otherwise agree.

16. Notice to Arbitrator of Appointment — Notice of the appointment of the neutral arbitrator shall be mailed to the arbitrator by the AAA and the signed acceptance of the arbitrator shall be filed with the AAA prior to the opening of the first hearing.

17. Disclosure by Arbitrator of Disqualification — Prior to accepting the appointment, the prospective neutral arbitrator shall disclose any circumstances likely to create a presumption of bias or that the arbitrator believes might disqualify him or her as an impartial arbitrator. Upon receipt of such information, the AAA shall immediately disclose it to the parties. If either party declines to waive the presumptive disqualification, the vacancy thus created shall be filled in accordance with the applicable provisions of these rules.

18. Vacancies — If any arbitrator should resign, die, withdraw, refuse or be unable or disqualified to perform the duties of office, the AAA shall, on proof satisfactory to it, declare the office vacant. Vacancies shall be filled in the same manner as that governing the making of the original appointment, and the matter shall be reheard by the new arbitrator.

19. Time and Place of Hearing — The arbitrator shall fix the time and place for each hearing. At least five days prior thereto, the AAA shall mail notice of the time and place of hearing to each party, unless the parties otherwise agree.

20. Representation by Counsel — Any party may be represented at the hearing by counsel or by another authorized representative.

21. Stenographic Record — Any party wishing a stenographic record shall make arrangements directly with a stenographer and shall notify the other parties of such arrangements in advance of the hearing. The requesting party or parties shall pay the cost of such record. If such transcript is agreed by the parties to be, or in appropriate cases determined by the arbitrator to be, the official record of the proceeding, it must be made available to the arbitrator, and to the other party for inspection, at a time and place determined by the arbitrator.

22. Attendance at Hearings — Persons having a direct interest in the arbitration are entitled to attend hearings. The arbitrator shall have the power to require the retirement of any witness or witnesses during the testimony of other witnesses. It shall be discretionary with the arbitrator to determine the propriety of the attendance of any other person.

23. Adjournments — The arbitrator for good cause shown may adjourn the hearing upon the request of a party or upon his or her own initiative, and shall adjourn when all of the parties agree thereto.

24. Oaths — Before proceeding with the first hearing, each arbitrator may take an oath of office and, if required by law, shall do so. The arbitrator may require witnesses to testify under oath administered by any duly qualified person and, if required by law or requested by either party, shall do so.

25. Majority Decision — Whenever there is more than one arbitrator, all decisions of the arbitrators shall be by majority vote. The award shall also be made by majority vote unless the concurrence of all is expressly required.

26. Order of Proceedings — A hearing shall be opened by the filing of the oath of the arbitrator, where required; by the recording of the place, time and date of hearing and the presence of the arbitrator, the parties, and counsel, if any; and the receipt by the arbitrator of the Demand and answer, if any, or the Submission.

Exhibits may, when offered by either party, be received in evidence by the arbitrator. The names and addresses of all witnesses and exhibits in order received shall be made a part of the record.

The arbitrator may vary the normal procedure under which the initiating party first presents its claim, but in any case shall afford full and equal opportunity to all parties for the presentation of relevant proofs.

27. Arbitration in the Absence of a Party — Unless the law provides to the contrary, the arbitration may proceed in the absence of any party, who, after due notice, fails to be present or fails to obtain an adjournment. An award shall not be made solely on the default of a party. The arbitrator shall require the other party to submit such evidence as may be required for the making of an award.

28. Evidence — The parties may offer such evidence as they desire and shall produce such additional evidence as the arbitrator may deem necessary to an understanding and determination of the dispute. An arbitrator authorized by law to subpoena witnesses and documents may do so independently or upon the request of any party. The arbitrator shall be the judge of the relevancy and materiality of the evidence offered and conformity to legal rules of evidence shall not be necessary. All evidence shall be taken in the presence of all of the arbitrators and all of the parties except where any of the parties is absent in default or has waived the right to be present.

29. Evidence by Affidavits and Filing of Documents — The arbitrator may receive and consider the evidence of witnesses by affidavit, but shall give it only such weight as seems proper after consideration of any objection made to its admission.

All documents not filed with the arbitrator at the hearing, but arranged at the hearing or subsequently by agreement of the parties to be submitted, shall be filed with the AAA for transmission to the arbitrator. All parties shall be afforded opportunity to examine such documents.

30. Inspection — Whenever the arbitrator deems it necessary, he may make an inspection in connection with the subject matter of the dispute after written notice to the parties who may, if they so desire, be present at such inspection.

31. Closing of Hearings – The arbitrator shall inquire of all parties whether they have any further proofs to offer or witnesses to be heard. Upon receiving negative replies, the arbitrator shall declare the hearings closed and a minute thereof shall be recorded. If briefs or other documents are to be filed, the hearings shall be declared closed as of the final date set by the arbitrator for filing with the AAA. The time limit within which the arbitrator is required to make an award shall commence to run, in the absence of another agreement by the parties, upon the closing of the hearings.

32. Reopening of Hearings – The hearings may for good cause shown be reopened by the arbitrator at will or on the motion of either party at any time before the award is made, but, if the reopening of the hearings would prevent the making of the award within the specific time agreed upon by the parties in the contract out of which the controversy has arisen, the matter may not be reopened unless both parties agree upon the extension of such time. When no specific date is fixed in the contract, the arbitrator may reopen the hearings and shall have 30 days from the closing of the reopened hearings within which to make an award.

33. Waiver of Oral Hearings – The parties may provide, by written agreement, for the waiver of oral hearings. If the parties are unable to agree as to the procedure, the AAA shall specify a fair and equitable procedure.

34. Waiver of Rules – Any party who proceeds with the arbitration after knowledge that any provision or

requirement of these rules has not been complied with and who fails to state objection thereto in writing, shall be deemed to have waived the right to object.

35. Extensions of Time – The parties may modify any period of time by mutual agreement. The AAA for good cause may extend any period of time established by these rules, except the time for making the award. The AAA shall notify the parties of any such extension of time and its reason therefor.

36. Serving of Notice – Each party to a Submission or other agreement which provides for arbitration under these rules shall be deemed to have consented and shall consent that any papers, notices, or process necessary or proper for the initiation or continuation of an arbitration under these rules; for any court action in connection therewith; or for the entry of judgment on an award made thereunder may be served upon such party by mail addressed to each party or its attorney at the last known address or by personal service, within or without the state wherein the arbitration is to be held.

37. Time of Award – The award shall be rendered promptly by the arbitrator and, unless otherwise agreed by the parties or specified by law, no later than 30 days from the date of closing the hearings or, if oral hearings have been waived, from the date of transmitting the final statements and proofs to the arbitrator.

38. Form of Award – The award shall be in writing and shall be signed either by the neutral arbitrator or by a concurring majority if there be more than one arbitrator. The parties shall advise the AAA whenever they do not require the arbitrator to accompany the award with an opinion.

39. Award Upon Settlement – If the parties settle their dispute during the course of the arbitration, the arbitrator may, upon their request, set forth the terms of the agreed settlement in an award.

40. Delivery of Award to Parties — Parties shall accept as legal delivery of the award the placing of the award or a true copy thereof in the mail by the AAA, addressed to such party at its last known address or to its attorney; personal service of the award; or the filing of the award in any manner that may be prescribed by law.

41. Release of Documents for Judicial Proceedings — The AAA shall, upon the written request of a party, furnish to such party, at its expense, certified facsimiles of any papers in the AAA's possession that may be required in judicial proceedings relating to the arbitration.

42. Judicial Proceedings and Exclusion of Liability — (a) Neither the AAA nor any arbitrator in a proceeding under these rules is a necessary party in judicial proceedings relating to the arbitration. (b) Neither the AAA nor any arbitrator shall be liable to any party for any act or omission in connection with any arbitration conducted under these rules.

43. Administrative Fee — As a not-for-profit organization, the AAA shall prescribe an administrative fee schedule to compensate it for the cost of providing administrative services. The schedule in effect at the time of filing shall be applicable.

44. Expenses — The expense of witnesses for either side shall be paid by the party producing such witnesses.

Expenses of the arbitration, other than the cost of the stenographic record, including required traveling and other expenses of the arbitrator and of AAA representatives and the expenses of any witnesses or the cost of any proof produced at the direct request of the arbitrator, shall be borne equally by the parties, unless they agree otherwise, or unless the arbitrator, in the award, assesses such expenses or any part thereof against any specified party or parties.

45. Communication with Arbitrator — There shall be no communication between the parties and a neutral arbitrator other than at oral hearings. Any other oral or written communications from the parties to the arbitrator shall be directed to the AAA for transmittal to the arbitrator.

46. Interpretation and Application of Rules — The arbitrator shall interpret and apply these rules insofar as they relate to the arbitrator's powers and duties. When there is more than one arbitrator and a difference arises among them concerning the meaning or application of any such rule, it shall be decided by majority vote. If that is unobtainable, either arbitrator or party may refer the question to the AAA for final decision. All other rules shall be interpreted and applied by the AAA.

ADMINISTRATIVE FEE SCHEDULE

Initial Administrative Fee: The initial administrative fee is $100 for each party, due and payable at the time of filing. No refund of the initial fee is made when a matter is withdrawn or settled after the filing of the Demand for arbitration.

Additional-Hearing Fees: A fee of $50 is payable by each party for each second or subsequent hearing that is either clerked by the AAA or held in a hearing room provided by the AAA.

Postponement Fees: A fee of $40 is payable by a party causing a postponement of any scheduled hearing.

American Arbitration Association
Expedited Labor Arbitration Rules

(As amended and in effect July 1, 1986)

INTRODUCTION

In 1971, in response to the concern of parties over rising costs and delays in grievance arbitration, the Labor-Management Committee of the American Arbitration Association recommended the establishment of expedited procedures, under which cases could be scheduled promptly and awards rendered no later than five days after the hearings. In return for giving up certain features of traditional labor arbitration, such as transcripts, briefs and extensive opinions, the parties utilizing simplified procedures can get quick decisions and realize certain cost savings.

These expedited rules provide such a procedure for use in appropriate cases. Most leading labor arbitrators have indicated a willingness to offer their services under these rules, and the Association makes every effort to assign the best possible arbitrators with early available hearing dates. Since the establishment of these procedures, an ever increasing number of parties has taken advantage of them.

EXPEDITED
LABOR ARBITRATION

1. Agreement of Parties — These Rules shall apply whenever the parties have agreed to arbitrate under them, in the form obtaining at the time the arbitration is initiated.

2. Appointment of Neutral Arbitrator — The AAA shall appoint a single neutral arbitrator from its Panel of Labor Arbitrators, who shall hear and determine the case promptly.

3. Initiation of Expedited Arbitration Proceeding — Cases may be initiated by joint submission in writing, or in accordance with a collective bargaining agreement.

4. Qualifications of Neutral Arbitrator — No person shall serve as a neutral arbitrator in any arbitration in which that person has any financial or personal interest in the result of the arbitration. Prior to accepting an appointment, the prospective arbitrator shall disclose any circumstances likely to prevent a prompt hearing or to create a presumption of bias. Upon receipt of such information, the AAA shall immediately replace that arbitrator or communicate the information to the parties.

5. Vacancy — The AAA is authorized to substitute another arbitrator if a vacancy occurs or if an appointed arbitrator is unable to serve promptly.

6. Time and Place of Hearing — The arbitrator shall fix a mutually convenient time and place of the hearing, notice of which must be given at least 24 hours in advance. Such notice may be given orally.

7. Representation by Counsel — Any party may be represented at the hearing by counsel or other representative.

8. Attendance at Hearings — Persons having a direct interest in the arbitration are entitled to attend hearings. The arbitrator may require the retirement of any witness during the testimony of other witnesses. The arbitrator shall determine whether any other person may attend the hearing.

9. Adjournments — Hearings shall be adjourned by the arbitrator only for good cause, and an appropriate fee will be charged by the AAA against the party causing the adjournment.

10. Oaths – Before proceeding with the first hearing, the arbitrator shall take an oath of office. The arbitrator may require witnesses to testify under oath.

11. No Stenographic Record – There shall be no stenographic record of the proceedings.

12. Proceedings – The hearing shall be conducted by the arbitrator in whatever manner will most expeditiously permit full presentation of the evidence and arguments of the parties. The arbitrator shall make an appropriate minute of the proceedings. Normally, the hearing shall be completed within one day. In unusual circumstances and for good cause shown, the arbitrator may schedule an additional hearing within five days.

13. Arbitration in the Absence of a Party – The arbitration may proceed in the absence of any party who, after due notice, fails to be present. An award shall not be made solely on the default of a party. The arbitrator shall require the attending party to submit supporting evidence.

14. Evidence – The arbitrator shall be the sole judge of the relevancy and materiality of the evidence offered.

15. Evidence by Affidavit and Filing of Documents – The arbitrator may receive and consider evidence in the form of an affidavit, but shall give appropriate weight to any objection made. All documents to be considered by the arbitrator shall be filed at the hearing. There shall be no posthearing briefs.

16. Close of Hearings – The arbitrator shall ask whether parties have any further proofs to offer or witnesses to be heard. Upon receiving negative replies, the arbitrator shall declare and note the hearing closed.

17. Waiver of Rules – Any party who proceeds with the arbitration after knowledge that any provision or requirement of these Rules has not been complied with and who fails to state objections thereto in writing shall be deemed to have waived the right to object.

18. Serving of Notice – Any papers or process necessary or proper for the initiation or continuation of an arbitration under these Rules, for any court action in connection therewith, or for the entry of judgment on an award made thereunder may be served upon such party (a) by mail addressed to such party or its attorney at its last known address, (b) by personal service, or (c) as otherwise provided in these Rules.

19. Time of Award – The award shall be rendered promptly by the arbitrator and, unless otherwise agreed by the parties, not later than five business days from the date of the closing of the hearing.

20. Form of Award – The award shall be in writing and shall be signed by the arbitrator. If the arbitrator determines that an opinion is necessary, it shall be in summary form.

21. Delivery of Award to Parties – Parties shall accept as legal delivery of the award the placing of the award or a true copy thereof in the mail by the AAA, addressed to such party at its last known address or to its attorney; personal service of the award; or the filing of the award in any manner that may be prescribed by law.

22. Judicial Proceedings and Exclusion of Liability – (a) Neither the AAA nor any arbitrator in a proceeding under these Rules is a necessary party in judicial proceedings relating to the arbitration. (b) Neither the AAA nor any arbitrator shall be liable to any party for any act or omission in connection with any arbitration conducted under these Rules.

23. Expenses – The expenses of

witnesses for either side shall be paid by the party producing such witnesses.

24. Interpretation and Application of Rules — The arbitrator shall interpret and apply these Rules insofar as they relate to the arbitrator's powers and duties. All other Rules shall be interpreted and applied by the AAA.

FEE SCHEDULE

Administrative Fees: The initial administrative fee is $75.00 for each party, due and payable at the time of filing. No refund of the initial fee is made when a matter is withdrawn or settled after the filing of the Demand for Arbitration.

Additional-Hearing Fees: For each second and subsequent hearing which is either clerked by the AAA or held in a hearing room provided by the AAA, each party shall pay $50.

Postponement Fees: A fee of $40.00 is payable by a party causing a postponement of any scheduled hearing.

Citations

1. See BNA, Labor Arbitration Reports, 43LA1262
2. See Owen Fairweather, "Employer Actions and Options in response to Strikes in Breach of Contract," in Proceedings of NYU, 18th Annual Conference on Labor (Washington, DC: BNA, Inc., 1966)
3. Proceedings of National Academy of Arbitrators, Jan. 27, 1956
4. See 46LRRM2416
5. See 42LRRM2034
6. See 54LRRM1327
7. See 25LA300-301
8. See 32LA753
9. See 24LA453
10. See 22LA761
11. See 13LA747
12. See 43LA689
13. See 51LRRM2752 and 52LRRM2764
14. See 8LRRM1038
15. See 41LA76
16. See 44LA224
17. See 43LA337
18. See 32LA865
19. See 42LA1162. For additional cases involving production standards, see 41LA953, 32LA317, 42LA298 and 1127, 43LA1208.
20. See 28LRRM1579
21. See 10LRRM483
22. See 33LRRM2417
23. See 19LRRM2009
24. See 29LRRM2379
25. See 29LRRM1482
26. See 29LRRM2302
27. See 29LRRM2290
28. See 29LRRM1105
29. See 29LRRM2331
30. See, for example, 31LRRM2082
31. See 45LA515 and 42LA555
32. See 16LA616 and 32LA586
33. See 45LA1128, 24LA132, 43LA947
34. See 28LA330
35. See 23LA252
36. See 25LA736
37. See 52LA861
38. See 52LA677

39. See 21LA105
40. See 12LA641
41. See 21LA314
42. See 43LA400
43. See 40LA1084
44. See 45LA53
45. William O. Douglas, *An Almanac of Liberty* (Doubleday, Garden City, NY, 1954), pp. 178 and 372.
46. See 28LA829, 27LA128 and 21LA80
47. See 25LA709, 20LA50, 28LA226 and 19LA733
48. See 32LA293
49. See 41LA888
50. See 31LA832
51. See 25LA568
52. See 43LA838
53. See 44LA1043
54. See 29LA182, 21LA560, 17LA230
55. See 3ALAA68, 5-408—see also 19LA854 and 203; 14LA381 and 12LA207
56. See 31LA599
57. See 32LA153
58. See 41LA575
59. See 44LA254; see also 44LA507
60. See 22LA1210
61. See 45LA1007
62. See 32LA26
63. See 33LA174
64. See 44LA343
65. See 44LA921
66. See 44LA730
67. See 42LA298
68. See 42LA307
69. See 42LA412
70. See 41LA974
71. See 44LA565
72. See 44LA1139
73. See 24LA163, 1LA468, and 11LA1158
74. See 31LA567
75. See 41LA283
76. See 41LA796
77. See 43LA640
78. See 28LA891
79. See 44LA847
80. See 38LA1109
81. See 48LA189
82. See 35LA103
83. See 41LA591
84. See 30LA213
85. See 8LA837
86. See 8LA897
87. See 3LA786

88. See 4LA430
89. See 24LA48
90. See 21LA457
91. See 46LA1161
92. See 27LA512
93. See 53LA1214
94. See 45LA968
95. See 45LA1050
96. See 44LA428
97. See 44LA552
98. See 34LA636
99. See 39LA404
100. See 43LA242
101. See 64-2ARB8748
102. See 43LA900
103. See 45LA283
104. See 35LA227
105. See 28LA312
106. See 42LA504
107. See 44LA644
108. See 33LA902
109. See 38LA1185
110. See 43LA450
111. See 42LA923
112. See 4LRRM515
113. See 45LA366
114. See 45LA490
115. See 20LA749
116. See 34LA262
117. See 33LA112
118. See 10LA265
119. See 16LA307
120. See 6LA965
121. See 30LA41
122. See 34LA464
123. See 33LA174
124. See 33LA879
125. See 10LA75
126. See 8LA75
127. See 10LA355
128. See 33LA103
129. See 19LA43, 3LA779
130. See 35LA699
131. See 28LA782
132. See 8LA765
133. Bureau of National Affairs (BNA), Washington, D.C. 10007.
134. BNA. See *Labor Relations Reporter,* Sept. 1981.
135. BNA. See *Annual Proceedings of the National Academy of Arbitrators,* 1981.

Bibliography

Aaron, Benjamin. *The Future of Labor Arbitration in America.* New York: American Arbitration Association, 1976.

_____. *The Impact of Public Employment Grievance Settlement on the Labor Arbitration Process.* Los Angeles: University of California, Institute of Industrial Relations, 1976.

AFL-CIO. *AFL-CIO Manual for Shop Stewards.* Washington, D.C., 1982.

Ames, Lewis R. "Due Process in Disciplinary Procedure." *Labor Law Journal* 27, No. 2, February 1976.

Baderschneider, Earl R., and Miller, Paul F., eds. *Labor Arbitration in Health Care: A Case Book.* New York: Spectrum Publications, 1976.

Baer, Walter E. *Discipline and Discharge Under the Labor Agreement.* New York: American Management Association, 1972.

_____. *The Labor Law Journal,* October 1966.

_____. *Labor Relations Guidebook.* Kendall/Hunt Publishing, 1978.

Beall, Edwin F., Wickersham, Edward D., and Kienast, Philip. *The Practice of Collective Bargaining,* 4th ed. Homeward, IL: Richard D. Irwin, 1972.

Bernstein, Merton C. *Private Dispute Settlement.* New York: Free Press, 1978.

Boyce, Timothy J. *Fair Representation, the NLRB, and the Courts.* Philadelphia: The Wharton School, University of Pennsylvania, 1978.

Bureau of National Affairs. *Grievance Guide,* 5th ed. Washington, D.C.: Bureau of National Affairs, 1978.

_____. *Management Rights and the Arbitration Process.* Proceedings of the Ninth Annual Meeting of the National Academy of Arbitrators. Bureau of National Affairs, 1956.

Chamberlaw, Neil W. *Collective Bargaining.* New York: McGraw-Hill, 1951.

Coulson, Robert. *Labor Arbitration: The Insecure Profession.* Proceedings of the NYU Twentieth Annual Conference on Labor. Albany, NY: Matthew-Bender, 1967.

_____. *Labor Arbitration: What You Need to Know.* New York: American Arbitration Association, 1973.

Crawford, Donald. *Challenges to Arbitration.* Proceedings of the Thirtieth Annual Meeting of the National Academy of Arbitrators. Bureau of National Affairs, 1960.

Davey, Harold W. *Contemporary Collective Bargaining.* Englewood Cliffs, NJ: Prentice-Hall, 1972.

_____. *Improving Grievance Arbitration: The Practitioners Speak.* Ames, IA: Iowa State University, Industrial Relations Center, 1972.

Elkin, Randyl, and Hewitt, Thomas L. *Successful Arbitration: An Experiential Approach.* Reston, VA: Reston Publishing, 1980.

Elkowri, Frank, and Elkowri, Edna. *How Arbitration Works,* 3rd ed. Washington, D.C.: Bureau of National Affairs, 1973.

Fairweather, Owen. *Practice and Procedure in Labor Arbitration.* Washington, D.C.: Bureau of National Affairs, 1973.

Fleming, R.W. *The Labor Arbitration Process.* Urbana, IL: University of Illinois Press, 1965.

Fossum, John A. *Labor Relations: Development, Structure, Process.* Dallas: Business Publications, 1979.

Fuller, H.D. *The Adversary System.* New York: Vantage Press, 1961.

Glume, Raymond G. "What to Put into a Grievance Clause." *Journal of Collective Negotiations,* No. 3, August 1972.

Goldberg, Arthur J. *Management's Reserved Rights: A Labor Review.* Proceedings of the Ninth Annual Meeting, National Academy of Arbitrators. Bureau of National Affairs, 1957.

Harrison, Allan J. *Preparing and Presenting Your Arbitration Case.* Washington, D.C.: Bureau of National Affairs, 1980.

Hutchinson, John G. *Managing a Fair Days Work.* Ann Arbor: The University of Michigan, 1963.

Justin, Jules. *Arbitrability and the Arbitrator's Jurisdiction: Management Rights and Arbitration Process.* Bureau of National Affairs, 1956.

_____. *How to Manage a Union.* Industrial Relations Workshop Seminars, 1969.

Kagel, Sam. *Anatomy of a Labor Arbitration.* Washington, D.C.: Bureau of National Affairs, 1961.

Kochan, Thomas A., et al. *Dispute Resolution Under Fact-Finding and Arbitration: An Empirical Analysis.* New York: American Arbitration Association, 1979.

Landis, Brook. *Value Judgments in Arbitration: A Case Study of Saul Wallen.* Ithaca, NY: Cornell University, New York State School of Industrial and Labor Relations, 1977.

Lapp, John A. *Labor Arbitration, Principles and Procedures.* New York: National Foreman's Institute, 1946.

Marceau, Leroy. *Drafting a Union Contract.* Boston: Little, Brown, 1965.

National Academy of Arbitrators. *Proceedings of the Annual Conference on Labor Arbitration, 1948 Through Present.* Washington, D.C.: Bureau of National Affairs, 1948. 33 volumes through 1981.

Nolan, Dennis R. *Labor Arbitration Law and Practice in a Nut Shell.* St. Paul, MN: West Publishing, 1979.

Prasow, Paul, and Peters, Edward. *Arbitration and Collective Bargaining: Conflict Resolution in Labor Relations.* New York: McGraw-Hill, 1970.

"Procedural Arbitrability — A Question for Court or Arbitrator?" *Labor Law Journal,* December 1963.

Repas, Bob. *Contract Administration.* Bureau of National Affairs Books, 1984.

Ryder, Meyer S. "Problems and Issues Involving the Private Adjudication of Bargaining Unit Work Coverage Disputes." 14 *Labor Law Journal* 839, 1963.

Scheinman, Martin F. *Evidence and Proof in Arbitration.* Ithaca, NY: New York State School of Industrial Relations, 1977.

Schmertyg, Herbert. *When and Where the Issue of Arbitrability Can Be Raised.* Englewood Cliffs, NJ: Prentice-Hall, 1966.

Schoen, Sterling H., and Hilgert, Raymond L. *Cases in Collective Bargaining and Industrial Relations: A Decisional Approach,* 3d ed. Homeward, IL: Richard D. Irwin, 1978.

Seide, Katharine. *A Dictionary of Arbitration*. Dobbs Ferry, NY: Oceana Publications, 1970.

Shulman, H. "Reason, Contract and Law in Labor Relations." 1968 *Harvard Law Review.*

Slegel, Boaz. *Proving Your Arbitration Case*. Washington, D.C.: Bureau of National Affairs, 1961.

Slichter, Summer H. *The Impact of Collective Bargaining on Management*. Washington, D.C.: The Brookings Institute, 1960.

Spitz, John A., ed. *Employee Discipline*. Los Angeles: University of California, Institute of Industrial Relations, 1977.

Stone, Morris. *Employee Discipline Arbitration*. New York: American Arbitration Association, 1977.

_____, and Baderschneider, Earl R. *Arbitration of Discrimination Grievances: A Case Book*. New York: American Arbitration Association, 1974.

Teple, Edwin R., and Moberly, Robert B. *Arbitration and Conflict Resolution* (Unit Six of *Labor Relations and Social Problems*). Washington, D.C.: Bureau of National Affairs, 1979.

Tracy, Estelle R., ed. *Arbitration Cases in Public Employment*. New York: American Arbitration Association, 1969.

Trotta, Maurice S. *Arbitration of Labor-Management Disputes*. New York: AMACOM, 1974.

_____. *Handling Grievances: A Guide for Management and Labor*. Washington, D.C.: Bureau of National Affairs, 1976.

_____, and Bishop, Walter. *Grievance Handling for Foremen*. Ann Arbor: The University of Michigan, 1969.

Updegraff, Clarence M. *Arbitration and Labor Relations,* 3d ed. Washington, D.C.: Bureau of National Affairs, 1970.

United States Department of Labor. Bureau of Labor Statistics. *Grievance and Arbitration Procedures in State and Local Agreements*. Washington, D.C.: U.S. Government Printing Office, 1974.

Werne, Beryamew. *Administration of the Labor Contract,* 3 vols. Mundelein, IL: Callagahan, 1963.

Wirtz, Willard W. *Due Process of Arbitration, The Arbitrator and the Parties*. Bureau of National Affairs, 1958.

Zack, Arnold M., and Block, Richard I. *The Arbitration of Discipline Cases: Concepts and Questions*. New York: American Arbitration Association, 1979.

Arbitration Awards

Bureau of National Affairs, *Labor Arbitration Reports*. Washington, DC: Bureau of National Affairs, weekly reports, bound volumes published semiannually since 1946.

Commerce Clearing House. *Labor Arbitration Awards*. San Rafael: Commerce Clearing House, weekly reports, bound volumes published semiannually since 1946.

Industrial Relations Guide. Englewood Cliffs, N.J.: Prentice-Hall.

Labor Relations Press. *Labor Arbitration Index*. Fort Washington, PA: Labor Relations Press, 12 issues yearly, index published since 1970.

Public Personnel Administration: Labor Management Relations. Englewood Cliffs, N.J.: Prentice-Hall.

Index